Keep It Real

Original Creole Orchestra; 1909 W. M Johnson, Manager Bass; Freddie Keppard, Cornet; George Baquet, clarinet; Jimmy Palao, Leader and violin; W. M. Williams, guitar; Eddie Vincent, trombone; dink Johnson, drummer.

Keep It Real

The Life Story of
James "Jimmy" Palao
"The King of Jazz"

Joan Singleton

iUniverse, Inc.
Bloomington

Keep It Real
The Life Story of James "Jimmy" Palao "The King of Jazz"

iUniverse books may be ordered through booksellers or by contacting:

iUniverse
1663 Liberty Drive
Bloomington, IN 47403
www.iuniverse.com
1-800-Authors (1-800-288-4677)

Because of the dynamic nature of the Internet, any web addresses or links contained in this book may have changed since publication and may no longer be valid.

Any people depicted in stock imagery provided by Thinkstock are models, and such images are being used for illustrative purposes only.

Certain stock imagery © Thinkstock.

ISBN: 978-1-4620-0721-9 (sc)
ISBN: 978-1-4620-0722-6 (dj)
ISBN: 978-1-4620-0723-3 (ebk)

Library of Congress Control Number: 2011906011

Printed in the United States of America

iUniverse rev. date: 4/19/2011

Contents

Greetings to All

Celebrate over 100 Years of Jazz

I extend my Greetings to all who appreciate the honest efforts of those who attempt to make living more enjoyable and brighter; who love laughter and smiles and the good things that go with them and to those who will read and appreciate my efforts to keep Jazz alive!!!

Jazz is the music that leaves you grinning with delight. It touches the very soul with its instruments sobbing, sighing, laughing and rasping as each musician improvises and perfects each tune. The evolution of American Jazz Culture continues throughout the 20th Century and is best demonstrated in a new program that is on the rise called "Stolen Moments". This movement "emphasizes the ways in which Jazz has acted as a unifying force, bridging cultural, ethnic and economic differences; stimulating cultural fusions and new stylistic idioms; it exemplifies democratic ideals and influences other genres of music, both in the U.S. and abroad."

This book is simply a spontaneous outpouring of my personal love and knowledge of the great musical art form that has filled my years with joy and happiness. I have attempted to present the simple plain facts, incidents and reminiscences of James "Jimmy" Palao, leader of the Original Creole Orchestra, who first started spreading Jazz throughout the USA and who is believed to have first coined the catchy musical term, "Jaz". The events leading to the beginnings of Jazz have been researched and sorted through and placed in chronological order to give a clear picture of the life, musical career and importance of Jimmy Palao's contribution to Jazz.

The birth place of Jazz is New Orleans is known for its interesting beauty, charming architecture and unique culture. The people are warm and friendly, the history is enchanting and the food is outstanding. The city is bursting with celebrations, parties and music in the streets. Jazz is definitely alive, in the streets that bore, the roots of the music which have become America's greatest musical contribution to the world. Special commemoration goes to all Jazz musicians who have continued to develop, perform and spread Jazz as we together... celebrate over one hundred years of Jazz!!!

Preface

I write this book in honor of James Palao and his family. I came to know his wife, Armontine Palao as "Cookie" in 1961 this was the year I married her oldest grandchild, James Palao Singleton. "Cookie" her manners and her style reeked of old New Orleans charm. She told me, the week before meeting me, she had dreamed of a dark brown lady with keen features and this lady wore a hat. The lady told her she was my grandmother Florence and she also told her to look out for me and to take care of me. "Cookie" actually described my grandmother and her hat and a pearl hat pin. Which no one could have known about because I had kept it hidden away wrapped in tissue for many years She also told me I was family now and always to treat Jim's mother, Agatha Palao-Singleton, as I would my own Mother. "Cookie" was a very wise woman.

We stayed with her the first three months of our marriage which was a little difficult at times. However, we left her home on a good note with hugs, kisses and tears. I continued the next years in a good relationship with her. We talked weekly and she shared many stories of her life with her husband and tip bits about her children. Her daughter Clotilde Palao-Wilson was a delight and she and I would spend hours chattering on the phone.

Jim and I worked closely with Clotilde as we researched the history of Jimmy Palao ("Cookie's" husband). I also communicated by email with Lawrence Gushee as he was finishing the writing of Pioneers of Jazz. We can credit Lawrence Gushee for bringing Jimmy Palao and the Original Creole Orchestra to the forefront. He gave witness and evidence to his presence and the important role he played in being the first to travel and lead the members of the Original Creole Orchestra and spread Jazz through a forum that is seldom thought of being connected with Black Americans. Vaudeville, an industry where most of America top stars performed on stage. That's how these Americans of color were able to travel extensively, share their art form and avoid all of the ugliness of racism in America.

On August 22, 1979, Lawrence Gushee contacted Clotilde Palao in a letter directed from Richard Allen the curator of the Jazz Archive at Tulane and he was well received by two ladies Armontine and Clotilde Palao, who were eager to discuss Jimmy Palao's role in the history of Jazz. They shared a wealth of directed information, which usually leaves out the human element. It is my intention to give life to one of the most important bandleaders of all time and to give living character to the members of that band.

Armontine and Clotilde often regretted that they couldn't get the whole family interested in gathering information, even though they were all proud of Jimmy Palao's accomplishments. They tried countless times and James Palao Singleton (Jimmy Palao oldest grandson) and I were the only ones willing to do the hard work. I shall always appreciate the experience of being in the presence of these two great women. Cookie would always serve her special Gumbo dish for us and afterwards she would share a story with us about her husband. Clotilde's face would light up as she enthusiastically talked about her father. The more I learned about him and researched his relationship with the band members he had so skillfully selected. It became apparent, that these musicians style of playing the music he so loved was having a unique and overwhelming effect on the crowds that were following them. Jimmy was an innovative bandleader and composer; this new music was taking hold and influenced many musicians and bands from diverse genres. He, without his knowledge began tearing down racial barriers that had previously prevented Black artist from being heard. I found the research and reading of so many books and going through so many interviews somewhat exhausting and time consuming, but in the long run the discoveries were rewarding. Natalie Brooks (Jimmy Palao's oldest granddaughter) was extremely helpful in clearing up many significant details, birthdates etc.

Since the massive storm that hit New Orleans I have come to view its aftermath as a rebirth and perhaps the beginning of another path in realizing the importance of my research and collectibles pertaining to Jazz and the life of Jimmy Palao. The knowledge gained from the older musicians, comes from more than twenty years of research. This information was invaluable, along with the many stories and memories passed on by Jimmy Palao's loving wife. If I had not taken the time to put this book together, all could be lost and my conscience would not allow that to happen. This in itself would be a tragedy and a dishonor to those who I had come to love. My husband (James Palao Singleton) had a great love for Jazz and he carried his grandfather name with pride. For almost four decades my husband brought Jazz into my life on a daily basis. We traveled to the Jazz festivals and every time there was a Jazz artist in Chicago we went to see them. Miles Davis, John Coltrane, Theolodius Monk, the names go on and on… He shared his views and critiques of the musicians and their performances with his Jazz aficionado's Raymond Head and Walter Clark. It was really very amazing listening to these guys and their enthusiastic monologues about the Jazz greats.

Perhaps the spirit of my husband James Palao Singleton and that of Jimmy Palao and his family are ultimately directing me through the next phase of my life. Once again, history and tradition have given me a sense of hope and direction for the future. I have often considered the philosophy of the New Orleans Jazz funeral—of sadly grieving the loss of life and joyously celebrating the beginning of its glorious resurrection. My old life has ended, but a new one has begun. We are always able to start over to learn, renew and rebuild.

Acknowledgements

Joan Lee Copy Editor:
Keep It Real

I take this moment to talk about mother daughter relationships. I have for months worked diligently on this book. I thought I should get someone to edit the information I had gathered. As I continued working and finally began to see the fruits of my labor unfold. I realized I might need someone to check the grammar, and to see that the all the i's are dotted and all the t's are crossed, in other words I needed a copy editor. Well after interviewing a few, I was at a lost they all seemed so eager to please me. This isn't what I needed; I guess I needed someone to critique my work.

One day my daughter entered the house. She was giving her view point on a specific issue, well do not always agree. In my artistic mind it is important for me to paint the picture as I see it and I don't get along well with controlling people. It dawned on me she is not scared to tell me how she feels, she is not scared to find fault with me or herself, she knows I will always love her and she loves to challenge me. As long as she always remains respectful I can live with the differences. I said "why don't you edit the book that I have been writing about your Great, Great, Grandfather? She said "I would be happy to but you won't give me a copy." I smiled. My mind reflected back on a conversation we had, that I summed up with, "It takes you too long to read a book." She continued,

"My job entails that I proof read a lot of the material. After all many in high positions have to read through my written transcripts.

Well to my surprise she grabbed the manuscript and without a word she was making notes and finding all of the flaws. I had found a copy editor! She worked through the night. In a week's time she had completed going through the book.. We never argued because we seldom spoke she just made notes and corrections. She is more direct and to the point than I am and sometimes I can become quiet wordy. If given time I do get to the point. Her corrections were well received. She had done a wonderful job. I can't thank her enough.

Let me tell you a little about Joan Singleton-Lee. In her youth she played the violin and piano. She is a young professional woman, in Social Services. She married divorced and raised her two children on her own. After she completed this undertaking she realized she had skills that she has been perfecting for years.

All events and people are set in place for special souls to enter this world at a certain place and time. They follow a direct path and no matter what the circumstance they can't be stopped until their mission is complete. They go against all the odds. Everything is suddenly set in motion, the correct people, the right moment and with a driving force they have an lasting impact that will bring a change in the world. We have witnessed this phenomenon time after time.

Introduction

James "Jimmy" Palao deservedly earned the title as the "First most important Orchestra leader from New Orleans" to spread Jazz throughout American and Canadian cities. It is my intention to bring forth the monumental steps taken by James "Jimmy" Palao, who had the courage to lead the Original Creole Orchestra traveling and introducing America's most valid form of music, Jazz... to the West and the East and the North. Jazz is one of the few great movements of an art that is truly an American phenomenon. It was born here in the United States. Jazz is one of the greatest cultural achievements created in the world and gives a powerful voice to the American experience. This music is born of a multi hued society of Black Americans from New Orleans. This music unites people across the divide of race, region and national boundaries. Jazz is still a profound manifestation of freedom, creativity, talent, achievement, and identity at home and abroad.

This book is dedicated to the life of one who played a major pivotal role in the development of Jazz. There is no denying the truth, James "Jimmy" Palao has been mentioned in book after book and in oral and written interviews by the world's foremost Jazz critics and scholars and by the men who helped create Jazz. I have simply complied all of the facts found in libraries, museums and from historical collections. Jimmy Palao was leader of the Original Creole Orchestra and he along with six other musicians traveled and shared their God-given talents and artistry through their music in cities across the United States and Canada.

Quite often historical accounts excluded people of color due to prejudiced attitudes those who initiated or changed the course of history were often overlooked. James Palao was first exposed to the style of improvisation from the Buddy Bolden solo method of playing his instrument in the middle of a tune. Jimmy as leader of the Imperial Orchestra and the Original Creole Orchestra went a step further and introduced and developed the style of collective improvisation with a syncopated 4/4 beat. He would 'star' the individual band members as they soloed and improvised and showcased their individual musical skills and talents...

Jimmy Palao had grown up and worked with most of the members of the Original Creole Orchestra since they were young. He had heard them in staging battles. He knew the aspects of their natural talent, musical background, ear training, memory retention, logic, reasoning and spirituality. They had all come from the same musical environment. He loved listening to them play their instruments. He wanted everyone to sway to the beat and enjoy their music. So as leader of the band he took a back seat and let each band member be heard at their best and gain individual fame. What a revelation! Jimmy Palao would take each of the band member's strongest tunes and allow them to let go, to edit, flip and riff the melody. What tremendous Sounds! These were the sounds of Jazz!!!

Jimmy was passionate about this style of music which allowed him to develop improvisation. Each soloist could star and expound upon the musical differences and similarities and each composition was brilliantly executed! It is certain that these were a new breed of musicians. They were breaking new ground, under the leadership of Jimmy Palao who encouraged the diverse repertoire and the employment of such wonderful mind-boggling techniques... Jazz musicians no longer had to stage battle one another to be heard and for crowds to roar. They were coming together as one band and each individual solo complimented the entire musical composition. The skilled performer or should I say soloist interpreted a tune in individual ways, never playing the same composition exactly the same way twice. This was the free style of music and the audience loved it. They ate it up. This was improvisation at its best. This style is what made Jazz... Jazz... Let it be noted that from all accounts Jimmy Palao was the first to call this music style "Jazz." (Evidenced; Jimmie Palao business card – 1908 and 1914).

The photographs are pictures of a window into time and place and give historical evidence to the facts presented in this book. The historical accounts are an evaluation of gathered evidence and certainly will draw obvious conclusions to edify the structuring of Jazz. Unfortunately many of the photographs were taken by people not in the photograph business. The conditions of these photographs are not always good. They were published and then distributed at the time they were taken and used for advertisement. I guess even the fact that they still exist or that there are copies of them is amazing for they are all nearly one hundred years old or older. A few of the photographs that were rarely seen come from the James Palao Singleton Family album. The narratives and summaries are based on testimony of musicians who witnessed and experienced many of the events that led to the development of Jazz. You will read insightful thoughts from many serious musicians and scholars who loved and respected this music. This book highlights obstacles faced by those who first dared to travel and spread Jazz as it gained national recognition. This was the beginning stages of developing the style of music called Jazz! I hope this book will arouse your curiosity it certainly has opened my eyes. I wanted to find out more about… how Jazz spread throughout the world without the presence of audio visual machines.

For most of the thousands of people who heard it, the Original Creole Orchestra was the first to communicate the exciting sounds of early Jazz from New Orleans. This band was good enough to make its way in shows that were otherwise exclusively white. Jimmy Palao was brave enough to withstand the prejudiced views of the times. He was daring enough to enter the dives, the joints, the honkytonks, the "barrel houses" and the "buckets of blood" and take Jazz to a height that rose to circuit tours and establishments of respect. Contained in this book are pictures and information of places, times, and facts. There were perhaps many overlooked, yet important events that may have had influence on the music that set the world on its feet.

Jazz history, by its very content, offered a dialogue of musical terms and cultures and various events that were seldom if at all mentioned. I hope the historical facts will generate interest in Jazz for the foreseeable future. There is still much research and information in the books, museums just waiting to be revealed. "History is like a vast ocean and no one can claim to know it all. The more you know, the more you realize how little you know. It is an eternal and infinite quest." I know of no other single art form more calculated to excite discussion and that will cover so many aspects of Jazz and its beginnings.

Throughout the text you will notice the word Jazz is Capitalized. The word 'Jazz' is, in most cases, a proper noun, and should be capitalized. However, if it is used in a colloquial context, such as "all that jazz" it is a common noun and should not be capitalized. Proper grammar is a mark of respect. Jazz has earned that recognition. We all should agree to write America's National Treasure "Jazz" with an upper case J... Resolution 57 was written and introduced by the Honorable, U.S. Congressman, John Conyers Jr. On September 1987 Resolution 57 designating Jazz as a "National American Treasure" passed the House of Representatives and the Senate. It begins by saying; Whereas, Jazz has achieved preeminence throughout the world as an indigenous American music and art form, bringing to this country and the world a uniquely American musical synthesis and culture through the African-American experience. As Jimmy Palao and the original Creole band were spreading their joyful sounds, little did these seven Jazzmen know what they were giving to the world. Wow! What an accomplishment for America!

I would like to credit every major source that freely gave and left the preserved historical Jazz accounts and data contained in the contents of this book. Much of the biographical information has been supplied by the musicians themselves, all of whom have died. I have relied mostly upon those who lived over a hundred to 75 years ago, during the period of 1875-1928. I gathered information from the stored collections, interviews and memories of well known Jazz players. Without their documented words and memories this book would not have been possible. Unfortunately some information was lost with the deaths of many musicians. I also must mention the loving memories that contributed to this work from the wife of Jimmy Palao, Armontine Carter-Palao, and his daughters Clotilde Palao-Wilson, Agatha Palao-Singleton and Jimmy Palao's oldest grandson, James Palao Singleton Sr. who along with me did extensive research, and Jimmy Palao's oldest granddaughter, Natalie Brooks (she corrected dates and spelling of family members names) and the great grandchildren Joan Lee the Copy Editor of this book and the continued support of Scott Singleton and

Breawnna Alexandria Lee who launched the Jimmy Palao video and the support from Steven Singleton, and William Singleton Sr. and the warmth and love generated through the years from Phillip Lee Jr. and William Singleton Jr. It would be impossible to write a book of this magnitude without the mention of, James Palao Singleton Jr. Diane Brooks, Shana Hampton. It is the sweet tones in memory from these magnificent people that have helped me to write this book. Nothing is worthy of being accomplished without love. Corinthians 13 4-7

You will read about the times, the challenges, obstacles, struggles that these Jazz musicians faced, by telling it like it really happened… and as James Palao often shouted to the band members… "Bring it on home… Keep It Real!" or "Talk to me baby… Keep It Real!"

Chapter One

New Orleans the Home of Jazz

We can't talk about Jazz without talking about New Orleans. One is synonymous with the other, the subjects are inseparable. Jazz could only have happened in New Orleans, the climate, the location, the structure of the city, the combining of cultures; recruiting of the brass bands during the Spanish American War. The Original Creole Orchestra, led by James "Jimmy" Palao and the breaking of racial barriers; it took all these factors and events from New Orleans to bring forth the birth and spreading of Jazz which became the most recognized musical art form… from the United States of America The Jazz musicians and Jazz journalists began to struggle for attention after Hurricane Katrina when historical interest in New Orleans began reaching its peak. Just when Jazz was becoming a diluted subject it resurfaced. A musical icon, Jimmy Palao, leader of the Original Creole Orchestra emerged along with William Manuel Johnson, Freddie Keppard, Eddie Vincent, George Baquet, Dink Johnson and Norwood or W.M. Williams.

Jazz, more than any other musical genre, is currently dominating academic presses. Judging from the deluge of recent books on Jazz the music shelf's life is just beginning. A movie is in progress about the man Buddy Bolden, the "Father of Jazz." According to historical accounts it was James Palao who originally taught Buddy Bolden, how to read music. Jimmy later played in the Buddy Bolden Band and he was impressed by the style of music which Buddy Bolden played. Jimmy became leader of the Imperial Band and developed this style of music.

1

Jimmie gathered musicians and formed the Original Creole Orchestra and traveled with this music he called "Jazz" .as it gained national prominence.

I found it necessary to visit New Orleans the place where Jazz originated and to research the circumstances and culture that brought forth this musical art form. New Orleanians have proven time after time that they can rise above all things: human plaques, fires and devastating floods. It is the character, the personality, the culture and the souls of the people that give them the desire to move beyond all obstacles. No matter what they face you always hear the energy in their music; the music that seems to give them the strength to keep moving on.

It is not my intention in the following statements to in any way romanticize slavery. The horrible humiliation of racism and the effects could have crumbled and crushed most people. According to historical accounts in the early 1800's many slaves lived on their own, in New Orleans; making a living at various jobs, and they were sending home a few dollars to their owners in the country they were from. The New Orleans Code Noir or Black Code required masters to allow slaves to rest on Sunday, permitted marriage and allowed owners to free slaves.

In 1803 there were nearly three thousand free slaves in New Orleans. Also abused slaves could legally sue their masters and win property and freedom. Affairs between the races were socially accepted. In New Orleans the men claimed their children and gave them their names, provided living quarters and took care of their children In addition a minority of wealthy white men permitted "placage" The status and life style of these mistresses were unique they were provided an elaborate wardrobe and lived in great houses in the Vieux Carre' (also known as the French Quarter) and any resulting children were supported and willed upon death to be free. Some were allowed to have balls in their master's homes, others were able to save and buy their freedom. Beginning in 1835 one day a week they were allowed to celebrate with dance and music. The "Place de Negroes", which was later known as Congo Square began in 1835. It became the only place in the United States where slaves and all people gathered in masse to sing, play their instruments and dance. It was also where they would first begin to celebrate Mardi Gras. Something magnificent was happening in New Orleans... Mardi Gras was beginning to attract people from all over the world and a new music was beginning to fill the air. During the late 1800's and the early 1900's Mardi Gras celebrations were filled with music, elaborate decorations, people dressed in costumes, parades, picnics, floats, excitement, entertainment, celebrity guests, it is now the biggest holiday in New Orleans. Everyone wears the colors of purple, green, and gold. Beaded necklaces are thrown from the beautiful floats and elaborate decorated balconies. All of the roads are practically shut down -- people are walking everywhere kids are everywhere, and they love it!

Most people from Louisiana boast of a varied lineage with branches that extend into Europe and Africa. The free Blacks of New Orleans were considered a highly cultured class who enjoyed a higher quality of life than Blacks anywhere else in the United States (and even many whites in the US didn't live as well). The "Crescent City" - so called because it was built along a bend in the river and was also home to Choctaw and Natchez Indians. It became open to an influx of people: the West African, Haitian, Barbadians (Bajans) and Balkans: Dalmatians, Serbs, Montenegrins, French, Spanish, Greeks, and Albanians. Spanish-speaking Filipinos came and stayed, too, alongside Chinese and Malaysians. After 1850, large numbers of Italians, German and Irish and Sicilian immigrants would be added to the mix. They each brought their culture and music with them. New Orleanians were all living together, in harmony in New Orleans, ("New Awlins" as pronounced by the local citizenry).

This rich mix of cultures in New Orleans resulted in considerable cultural exchange. A rare city that with various ethnic groups, who for the most part got along with one another. After research I concluded that New Orleanians, although not perfect, showed from their very beginnings that if various cultures share and appreciate what the other brings to the table that something new and better, can and will and… emerge. An early example was the city's relatively large and free Creole community. Creoles were people of mixed African and European blood and were often well educated in music, crafts and trades. Creole musicians were particularly known for their skill and discipline. Many played in the best orchestras in the city and they individually traveled throughout the city to teach and share their talents.

New Orleans is unique in American history in that music was and still is a major part of everyday life. It is called "The City of Music". A poet unknown to me once said "New Orleans City hums during the day and sings at night". Not only were there brass bands for all occasions (parades, parties, celebrations, and funerals), but most corners had street musicians and singers, willing to entertain for pennies. No day goes by without live music being heard.

New Orleanians loved to dance. Dance halls were plentiful during the early 1900's, the most popular were the Economy Hall, Friends of Hope Hall (Treme Street), Globe Hall (St. Charles and St. Peter Street) Geddes Hall, Good Intent Hall (in Algiers), Longshoreman's Hall (Jackson Street) Masonic Hall, Mississippi River Hall, St. Peters Hall (Cadiz and Coliseum St.), Screwmen's Hall (Burgundy and Bagatelle Street), Veterans Hall, Union Hall. The dances were given by a proliferation of social clubs. The patrons were charged admission at the door of 15 cents or 25 cents. Business was good, there were so many clubs booked for dancing that they barely had time to clear the floor.

New Orleans is clearly the only city in the world with the incredible conditions and energy that was needed to sprout the beginning seeds of Jazz. New Orleans is the City of Jazz, of Creole culture and of a relaxed good way of life. The great city of New Orleans has stayed very old in its beliefs of, food, music, and even church, government, and many festivities. They have retained the ways of the Creole nation and they spoke Catholic French instead of English. New Orleans is the kind of place where people are more rested and they have a very easy going spirit. The pace of life moves slowly, people laugh and love easily. The climate is filled with a lot of excitement and merriment.

The people of New Orleans were warm and friendly and that good old Southern hospitality still exists today. Every time we visited New Orleans we were welcomed into homes and doors were opened to us and we were served well. New Orleans is also a city of restaurants and they line the city streets and are known for great dishes like Gumbo, Jambalaya, Red Beans and Rice, fried sea foods, or a Po-Boy sandwich. The old neighborhoods date back centuries and have alluring interesting structures. The families have grown together, raised their children together, shared weddings, births, funerals and every event that encompassed their lives. All of the people we met spoke freely of their good times together. They were eager to reminisce and share their stories and experiences with us. It seems the sounds of music surrounded every celebration of their lives and stayed in their memory. It became clear that this was the only place that could create a new American music. A music that makes people feel free, it made people feel alive! As I traveled the streets of New Orleans I felt the vibe, it was easy to become absorbed by the hot and lyrical sounds from the musical instruments. This music makes people want to move their bodies to the beat and nobody can play it like they play it in New Orleans. The sounds seem to resonate through your entire body washing tensions and worries away. New Orleans, a city alive and vibrant, a city that musically expresses joy and sorrow, a city where you could dance down the middle of the street, in the middle of the daytime, and people would join you. The glory of New Orleans is that… it's still that way today.

New Orleanians learned to play musical instruments that their ancestors from the old world brought with them to the New World. One instrument that they especially had an affinity for was the violin. They combined African music with the violin carrying the melody and created dances that blended with the sounds they produced.

The love of music in all of New Orleans became so popular that the people started having even more festivals to celebrate their great land and city. New Orleans was not without its problems. The great fires of 1788 destroyed 856 of the 1,100 structures and in 1794 destroyed 212 structures in New Orleans. Mosquitoes plagued the residents with Yellow Fever and resulted in an unusually high death rate. More than 41,000 people died from the scourge of yellow fever in New Orleans between the years 1817-1905. New Orleanians have always managed to rebound with the energetic vitality that they are known for. All who lived in New Orleans were encouraged to join Benevolent Societies, where, aside from societal connections, they were assured a burial plot and a brass band to play at their funerals. Out of the sorrow of death came a proliferation of Brass and Jazz bands that still flourish in the city.

In my minds memory, the living landscapes of this city are almost musical in movement; the different hues of the people and the rhythm of the bouncing bodies in vivid colored clothes. The southern tropical breeze that brushes against your face and through your hair and whispers softly in your ears, is a constant reminded of the rhythm in the air. The moving swaying silhouettes, walking through the bright colored houses of the French Quarter or along wide boulevards of the Garden District are constant. Then there's the musical sounds of insects each vibrating with polychromatic fluttering and the songs of birds mating and chirping in the trees, the peaceful flowing sound of handmade waterfalls and the sounds of the music with a little a mix of Jazz and Blues. The smells are intoxicating; it is believed that in southern states, the flowers reach their height of scented power before they die. The strongest most pungent odors of flowers are present in New Orleans. In the evenings I smelled an occasional scent of Jasmine flowers in this wispy tropical New Orleans breeze. You'll get a sudden sniff of the Cajun foods cooking as you near the restaurants. There is a humid dampness in the air at times, perhaps that comes from the alligator spiked swamps that surround New Orleans.

Voodoo is still practiced in New Orleans. We were told stories of ghost, curses and haunted areas in New Orleans. I didn't take any of the haunted tours. I really didn't wish to disturb the spirits… In New Orleans, old homes are architectural treasures. You will see plantations, a garden district, Creole cottages, shotgun homes, colonial townhouses, and French, Spanish and Greek mansions. We walked through history with a walk down St. Charles Avenue, home to some of the city's most beautiful houses. From graceful verandas to elegant parlors, New Orleans' historic homes and buildings are beyond compare. The sound of music fills the air day after day. Jazz personifies a natural expression of the New Orleans culture.

Jazz… changed the landscape of America… and was the sound that put New Orleans on the map, musically speaking!!! (1)

Picture taken in 1967, with Singleton Kodak camera. Print distributed to several tourist. James Palao Singleton standing wearing a white shirt and Ivy League cap in New Orleans [Smith, Palao Singleton Family Tree Album

Chapter Two

James "Jimmy" Palao's Beginnings: Descent, Legacy and Culture

It was this history of combining and mixing the cultures and traditions that brought forth the birth of James A. Palao February 19, 1879 across the Mississippi in Algiers, New Orleans, Louisiana. In the Census Felix Palao, (James "Jimmy" Palao's father) was listed as a slave (web root, ancestry.com), the year of birth is incorrect: the 1900 census gives the correct year of birth as 1860. His mother is listed as an unknown African female with a possible name, Delarosa.

"In the 1840's through the 1880's the city had a prosperous class of free black and Creole entrepreneurs and skilled laborers in all fields. Thousands of slaves lived on their own in the city, and they made a living at various jobs, and send a few dollars or what they owed to their owners in the country they came from each month.

The question becomes how Felix Palao could be considered a slave and his mother and or father or sister or brothers were not listed as slaves? Due to the antebellum laws for integrated relationship if he was born from a Black woman he would automatically become a slave. An act of Miscegenation carried out in New Orleans. The promulgation of the "one-drop theory," served as a political tool throughout the antebellum period of the United States because it could classify any person with one black ancestor as a slave.(2) Edouard Palao was Felix natural father and Marie Madeline Perrault his step mother both loved and raised him. Edouard's mistress was a Black woman and we do not know her full name, according to the family records she died a month or two after Felix was born. Felix was later listed in the census as a Creole. Creole once was only the language spoken by the French. Creole a term now designated to the people born from a mixed relationships native to New Orleans Louisiana. The mixed and multihued people of the state of New Orleans were descendants of the French, Spanish, Native American and African. These biracial relationships were not treated with such respect anywhere else in the US.

They celebrate their ethnic identity in a very different fashion. They are proud of who they are. They don't want to pass for anyone except who they are. They have their own language, literature, religion, art, food, music, folklore, professions, customs and social dignity. The term "Creole" means many things to many people. In current affairs usage, Creole is the language spoken by Haitians. In New Orleans, Creole has a long and distinguished heritage and culture. To be Creole is more of a culture and a social acceptance in New Orleans, Louisiana of biracial relationships than an ethnicity.

In order to respect and make sense of the underlying forces of Jimmy Palao's life and the people around him it became necessary to discover and understand how his life related to his teachings... his culture I researched the time period and the culture of the Creoles in the 1900's. The Creole culture and traditions concerning "extracurricular and extramarital activity" were that most of the young male Creoles had mistresses... If they did not, it could be considered a reflection upon their manhood. Abstinence was no virtue, and a dark mistress was as much a mark of social distinction as the possession of fine horses and carriages... The Creole men were given their own quarters for entertainment purposes. The single men had mistresses who were Black or Mulatto, It was not unusual for a young white Creole man to take a free woman of color as his mistress. Set her up in her own house and have several children with her before he reached his mid to late twenties and marry a French woman to raise his legitimate family. In New Orleans placage, did not involve slave women but rather free black women who had a limited degree of choice as to whether they were to become a mistress and whose mistress they would be. The relationship was often a long-lasting one, sometimes continuing long after the man married. Children born in placage generally took their white father's last name, were supported by him, and even in some cases indirectly inherited large sums upon his death. A married man having a mistress was an accepted custom because marriages were usually business arrangements, not for love, and the men expected their wives to be passive and faithful and loyal to them. The tradition in the Creole family is that the father was dominant. His word was law. He ruled his house like a king. The woman always held her position in the family as wife and mother.

In the late 1800's and early 1900's New Orleans, the Creoles were the economic, social, and cultural leaders.(2) They were considered to be the upper class and urbane city dwellers. They spoke French, educated their children in classical music instructions. They also clung to traditions, most were Catholic and considered themselves far superior to any other residents of New Orleans. They enjoyed a privileged lifestyle. In Louisiana, the term Creole came to represent children of black or racially mixed parents as well as children of French and Spanish descent with no racial mixing. In the words of Mother Henriette Delille when canonized she will have the distinction of being the first Creole Saint to have been born in New Orleans. She respects the cultural existence of the Creole people. She states in her written essay titled "No Cross, No Crown, Outline Mother Delille's Creole Ancestry" "… again, we are a melting pot of all races. Creole are multi-hued, they are fair, light dark and all shades. Creole denotes culture not color."(3)

Edouardo Palao owned a cigar store in New Orleans at the corner of Chartres and Hospital. Cigar making was a respectable source of work for many Creoles. Cigar connoisseurs had many opportunities, from a Cigar Factory to wonderful Cigar Bars. New Orleans is the nearest city to Havana and is the importer of most of Havanna crops sold in this market. It is the point of export of the tobacco crops of Kentucky and Ohio. At one time New Orleans was the largest and most important tobacco market in the world. Its cigars have gained and maintained a worldwide reputation and New Orleans still has the largest cigar factory, the Hernsheim factory.(4) There was a certain aura of sophistication about men who hand-rolled cigars. Cigar stores were gathering places for men of distinction. Edouardo Palao passed the cigar store on to Felix in later years.

Felix Palao Picture Dated 1920
(J.Singleton Family Tree Album)

Picture dated 1882 Clotilde
Rebbeca Spriggs-Palao [Singleton
Family Tree Album

Felix Palao married Clotilde Rebecca Spriggs October 18, 1878 in St Mary's Catholic Church, New Orleans, Louisiana. James (Jimmie) A. Palao was born from their union February 19, 1879 and he was baptized February 29, 1880.(5) It is customary for the parents and God parents of the child being baptized in the Roman Catholic Church to adopt the name of a saint who lived a great spiritual life and who enjoyed a very special relationship with the Lord Jesus. The saint's name is often used in conjunction with the child's middle name, but is not recognized in civil law. James took the name of Saint Florestan. His baptismal name was James Florestan Palao and he was born in the home of his grandparents, where his father (Felix-Palao) and his mother (Clotilde Rebecca Spriggs-Palao) lived. His mother died an early death in 1884. According to her death certificate she died of epilepsy. (Again this subject is too time consuming. Perhaps someone can look into the validity of this. I did briefly go on the internet database and in a few seconds I found several instances of death associated with epilepsy in the late 1800's.)

Algiers, New Orleans Louisiana,
(Family Album)

Jimmy Palao raised here 900
Verett, Algiers, New Orleans,
Louisiana [Family Album]

The family lived at 900 Verret, Algiers, New Orleans, Louisiana. (6) Clara Spriggs,(7) helped raise Jimmy along with his father Felix. He was the only child there and he was surrounded by female relatives.. Felix's heart poured out to Jimmy for he too had lost his Mother at an early age. Felix took a special interest in Jimmie's musical studies. His grandmother, Clara Spriggs, hired an aged woman to give him piano lessons in a group. When Felix began to instruct Jimmy he realized how talented his young six year old son was. He insisted Jimmy have private music lessons at least three times during the week for the next year. Jimmy received his musical training from this male German teacher who taught him how to read, write and play several instruments. Jimmy fell in love with the violin and he devoted most of the day to practicing and mastering the musical skills. For the next years he gave his youthful life to music.(8)

After the Civil War separate and unequal was the norm for New Orleans schools. In the 1878s -1910 funds from the estate of John McDonogh, a wealthy trader and slaveholder, began to construct schools, for predominantly poor children - specifically, white and freed black students. Black students were routinely restricted to lower grades and had no access to high school. The French were well educated and the Creole children born from these unions received the benefits of family and friends teaching them. The Palao's not only shared their educational training and skills with family they also went along the countryside to teach reading, math, writing and classical music.(9)

The Creole tradition was that music was quite often a family affair. Fathers and or family members passed on what they had learned down to sons, many of whom have risen to "stardom" on their respective instruments (Sometimes they played in the same band). Edgar Joseph Palao was the uncle of Jimmy and he taught him how to play the saxophone. Felix continued to live in Algiers but by 1889 moved across the river to the eighth ward, sharing quarters with his brother Vincent at 209 Spain St. At some point he fathered two children with a lady named Josephine, they were Felicia 1892, and Norman 1897, and both are recorded in the Palao Family Bible. The 1900 census however showed Josephine and Felix at the same address. A few years later Felix married Madeline Ferrand, Felix and Edgar Palao helped lay the groundwork for the path Jimmy Palao would take.(10) He almost worshipped the ground his father and uncle walked upon. Clotilde's Father told her, that his father and uncle took him and they traveled the country side in the evenings and as they rode up to the houses they could smell the delicious foods that were prepared for their coming. Felix and Edgar loved to talk and share and they taught music to anyone who was interested in learning."

The Excelsior Band Felix Kneeling next to tuba, marching band parade of Holy Name Society of Corpus Christi Parish, New Orleans Louisianna, January 19, 1917 [Donated to family Album by Modesta Palao

One day according a story told to Clotilde by her father, Uncle Edgar set Jimmy down and said "Jimmy you have a lot to offer so when you give a gift, let the gift you give be something that no one can take away and you will be greatly rewarded someday. You must practice your lessons over and over until you have learned all you need to know and you will then succeed in all you do". Jimmy said his uncle told some of the same stories over and over and he made him rehearse over and over. Sometimes after a lesson with Uncle Edgar, his father (Felix) would come and tell him to go to his room and rest. His father and uncle never argued even though they expressed opinions that were sometimes different. They almost studied each other before speaking their minds. Edgar had on several occasions had refused to participate in the violent battles between the bands; Edgar was a member of the Onward Brass Band. Felix and Edgar were both taught to play and read music and they were both skilled musicians.(11)

Around the year 1897 Jimmy began his playing the violin in the Sacred Heart of Mary's Hall on Valiiette at Evelina [streets] in New Orleans with his grandmother Clara Spriggs. This is when he also became know by some as Jimmie "Spriggs" Palao. According to Manuel Manetta, there were two bands in Algiers, Frankie Duson's and Buddy Johnson's: The Johnson Band always played at the Sacred Heart of Mary's Hall, Mrs. Spriggs a Creole lady high in the Sacred Heart Society, had gotten the job for her grandson. Jimmie Palao and he quickly became leader and violinist of the Johnson Band. Members of the all polite society attended the functions at the Sacred Heart of Mary's Hall.

Jimmy then went out on the road with his music. Armontine said Jimmy later told her, that he would go out to the country and give instructions to bands and get them started. According to Clara Spriggs one of Jimmy's students, whom he taught to read music, was to become the legendary - Charles "Buddy Bolden".(12) Around 1898 Jimmy Palao joined The Pacific Brass Band. This Brass Band may have come into existence on the demise of the Pickwick Brass Band. It began to decline as the Henry Allen Brass Band gained popularity. Charles Love remembers Jimmy Palao also played the mellophone in the Pacific Brass Band. Love said, "Palao was a first class violin and mellophone player. They tell me after he left here he learned to play the saxaphone".(13)

In 1898 Jimmy Palao joined the Henry Allen Brass Band, as his father had suggested. The band was based in Algiers. This was one of the city's finest reading Brass Bands and they played arranged marches and dirges as they were written. They adopted the grandiose custom of burying their dead in a manner similar to "full military honors" only they paraded and danced in the streets. They played for, conventions, festivals, concerts, weddings, airport greetings, receptions parties and any other function that warranted celebration. This was where Jimmy learned to play all sorts of line ups. Henry Allen's Brass Band was more than a marching band they could really swing. Jimmy learned quite a lot from Henry Allen and praised him to be "a very good conductor". The music performed by Henry Allen's Brass Band played a significant role in the development and style of music that Jimmy would later play. The instrumentation and section playing of the brass bands increasingly influenced the dance bands, which changed in orientation from string to brass instruments. What ultimately became the standard front line of a New Orleans Jazz band were the following instruments: the cornet, clarinet, and trombone. These horns collectively improvising or "faking" ragtime yielded the characteristic polyphonic sound of New Orleans Jazz. (14)

1898 – Henry Allen's Brass Band;: Algiers, Louisiana [5-44] Standing, Jack Carey, George Allen (?), Wallace Collins, Jimmy Palao, August Rousseau. Joe Howard, Oscar Celestin, Henry Allen Seated, Clay Jiles, George Sims, (Unknown)

I must deviate a little from Jimmy Palao to discuss the musical talent of Edgar Joseph Palao the brother of Felix Palao and uncle of Jimmy. Edgar played the clarinets occasionally with Charles Love in Plaquemine, Louisiana. His instrument limited him to one key because keys were built in on the transforming instruments. So he purchased a box of the older clarinets – D, C, E^b, A and B^b- to play with the band.(15) Due to Edgar Palao's position in the Onward Brass band, he and all the other band members were convinced by the recruiter to join the Ninth Infantry Immunes to fight in the Spanish American war. Very little mention is made of the Onward and Excelsior marching brass band's role in the Spanish War. Apart from vague references little is said about this curious and yet significant chapter in the New Orleans Brass Bands history. According to one source, the Excelsior and Onward Marching Brass Band gained considerable popularity during the 1880s. After the Civil War the Brass Military Bands became popular in the cities, these bands spared no expense for uniforms, flags, banners and instruments. These bands were territorial and if a band marched into another's district a contest ensued, where the two bands generally tried to out blow each other, creating a spectacle that drew crowds of delighted spectators. A lot of pride was at stake, these confrontations could sometimes get intense and violent. When things got out of hand, the instruments were put down and fist and knife fights ensued. The spectators would start running and screaming. The losing band was left with no alternative, but to flee the scene in humiliation. Many spectators and musicians were hurt and trampled to death.(16)

These events were happening at the same time of the Spanish-American War in the late 19th century. The Onward Brass Band had achieved a reputation as the number one toughest fighting marching brass band in New Orleans and The Excelsior Brass Band ranked number two. There was talk of white men forming a militia of their own. It was believed by the town's people that these warriors from the Brass bands were becoming strengthened in numbers and could pose a civilian threat to society. They were feared by some whites and politicians to be getting out of hand. It was thought by many whites that these bands might be constructing their own army. The bands were becoming a frightening force to many in the white community, who were armed and preparing to go against the violence. The last thing

America needed was a war among its own citizens. The Armed services were used not only to bring peace to other countries but to keep peace in America. Throughout the years it is evident that the Navy and armed forces have controlled many of the activities in New Orleans. Rightfully so, because New Orleans was and still is the base for many of the armed forces. Although seldom mentioned or perhaps overlooked, it is clear that the recruitment of band members into the Spanish American War by the US armed forces played a critical role in the orchestration of events or divine intervention leading to Jazz. A battle among civilians on the streets would have changed the whole musical climate of New Orleans.(17)

So, one might conclude that it was no coincidence, that in the summer of 1899, the U.S. War department issued an order to recruit Americans from New Orleans into the Ninth Volunteer Infantry Immunes. The regiment was called the "Immunes" because it was believed or used as a recruiting ploy that anyone with Black blood would be immune to diseases such as malaria and yellow fever. The recruiting was only for people of color and musicians, preferably the Onward and Excelsior band members.

On the day of departure the attendance and enthusiasm among the crowd was overwhelming. It seemed every Black American within 100 miles of New Orleans must have come to witness the departure of these troops. The Ninth Immune Infantry Regiment marched to the ship under the direction of their appointed band leader, James McNeil. Rumor spread that there were whites who planned to ambush the unit as they boarded the ship to Cuba. However, no attack ever materialized, perhaps because of the thousands and thousands of Black Americans who had turned out to see the troops board the ship.(18)

The August 18, 1898 New Orleans Daily Picayune, speculated that "The entire Black population of the city must have been present on the route from the fairgrounds to the wharf… everyone wanted to catch a glimpse of the Immunes. Just before noon the sound of music herald the approach of the awaiting multitude and a rush among the crowds was made for position to see the troops. The song of *"Dixie"* could be *heard* amidst the sounds of ear piercing wild cheers for ten minutes or more, one could hardly hear oneself think. The troops marched a mile and began boarding the Berlin ship which was 510 feet long."(19)

Spanish war Ninth Immune Infantry marching to board ship to Cuba; left James Mc Neil, middle second row; Edgar Joseph Palao, right; Ron (last name unknown)

Jimmy Palao remembered being sad and proud at the same time. His Uncle Edgar Joseph Palao was recruited. He was going to miss his Uncle and he was somewhat fearful he might not return. His Uncle had told him to take on his students. He taught the students just as his uncle would have wanted him to teach them. They would play over and over until the lesson was learned. This double load of students along with his other gigs kept Jimmy working from sun up to sun down. He'd always rush home from the countryside before dark. The roads could be a little dangerous at night.(20)

A peace treaty was signed April 1899. The Ninth Immune Infantry ended the Spanish American War with a few skirmishes and only five deaths. Most of their service time was spent in musical drills and guarding the prisoners. Ironically records indicate that incidence of malaria among the so-called immunes was actually higher than expected. September and October had been very difficult because the majority of the regiment came down with malaria and yellow fever. As a result the Ninth Immune Infantry experienced several deaths. There were no other casualties of war from this regiment. It seems the men never performed outside the unit. It was almost as though these men were recruited and brought together for a greater purpose ... They were drilled every day and were taught how to work and move as a team.

Many of the band members practiced on their instruments in isolation, When the entire band was put together the desired results to perform at maximum efficiency were achieved.(21) The drilling results increased in importance when men stopped fighting each other and began to work together as one unit. A sweet harmony was noticed among these once rivals who were now supporting one another. These men returned home with a new attitude toward one another and there were no more territorial fist or knife fights among them... only the well remembered call and response battles remained, which the crowds enjoyed. The musicians through the intense drill instructions, military exercises and intense physical training now shared a mutual camaraderie. The uniting of these men ended all feuding in the streets of New Orleans ... which seemly was headed toward the self destruction of the marching brass bands in New Orleans. This was clearly one of the first major steps of many more to come that paved the way for New Orleans music to become America's new art form.... On the day the regiment returned to New Orleans James McNeil, the master band director led the troops down Fifth Avenue in the Victory Parade with thousands of onlookers cheering for them.(22)

Upon the return of Edgar Palao, Jimmy was relieved of his responsibility to his uncle's students. A month or two later the Ninth Immune Infantry in a planned ceremony gathered on the grounds of the picnic area near Lake Pontchartrain. The participating musicians gave a spectacular performance in tribute to one another. According to Jimmy Palao he stood witness to this magnificent collaboration of talent. He looked at the faces in the crowd and listened to the sounds of the audience... He was blown away by the audible reactions to the performance, the laughter, applause, gasps, and shouts for more. This eventful moment had a lasting effect on Jimmy Palao which influenced and further heightened his musical aspirations. The sequences of these events were the beginning steps that paved the way for the musical career of Jimmy Palao. In 1904 Edgar Joseph Palao established a theatrical tour group called Bush's Ragtime Opera which he solely managed. (23) Jimmy Palao got a big kick out of playing the new ragtime music so he joined the touring group from time to time. These traveling musical companies provided opportunities for many talented trained musicians. His Uncle Edgar according to Jimmy seemed almost relentless in building friendships and sharing his talent with others... a lesson reinforced while he was in the armed forces. Jimmy Palao during this period according to Armontine felt he had learned and witnessed the most important lesson in life... to always share those gifts that couldn't be taken away. Edgar Joseph Palao died ten years later of natural causes. Jimmy Palao continued teaching all he learned to any musician that wanted instructions as his career path began to unfold...

Chapter Three

First Steps of Path to Jazz Career

Jimmy remembered meeting lots of people along the countryside. A few might have been relatives he wasn't sure. However he made lots of friends. He loved to go to the country, he said the people were so alive and friendly he always felt welcomed. The idea to travel remained prevalent in Jimmy Palao's mind. It wasn't unusual for a few of New Orleans musicians to travel around the city. Jimmy Palao found joy in sharing his musical talent and he ventured out a little further than he had with his uncle and father. He went out to the adjoining parishes and small towns and plantations along the Mississippi to offer instructions to new musicians and newly organized bands.

Due to the violins ability to stand out over other instruments, Jimmy found it to be perfect for playing a melody line at a high pitch. Jimmy Palao mastered and took control of the instrument. The violin has such vibrant tones and from this small instrument he rendered powerful sounds that eschewed vibrato phrasings and nobody had heard anything quite like it before.

Jimmy Palao had a network of youthful connections (childhood friends) some of which endured for his entire life. He played in various bands with these guys and he later featured them in the Original Creole Orchestra where Jazz began to gain worldwide fame: After he withdrew from the Henry Allen Sr. Band. Jimmie Palao formulated his own ensemble band in 1900. Rene Baptiste played the guitar and others doubled in his band from other bands. They played at the picnics, parties and parades on Lake Pontchartrain and played at saloons in Storyville and the French Quarter; they were heard playing all over town, on Rampart and Perdido streets, uptown, downtown, and across the river. Lake Pontchartrain which technically isn't a lake at all: it's an estuary, or a coastal body of water that has an open connection to a sea. Lake Pontchartrain is a calm beauty of green saltwater lapping against barnacle-covered pilings and it is bound by land, but one side is a marsh, which connects it to the Gulf of Mexico. It is the second largest salt water lake in the United States. Jimmy loved the playing along the beautiful lakeside. He was becoming well-known and he associated with some of the best-trained and naturally talented musicians. Jimmy had formed friendships with many well known and unknown band members.(1)

1900 – Jimmy Palao Band: left to right; Sitting: Edward "Chico" Claiborne - Trombone, Louis Rodriguez - Trumpet, Joe Smith - violin and Rene Baptiste - Guitar, Standing; James "Jimmy" Palao – Violinist, James Nuenutt - Bass Violinist, and Toby Nuenutt - Bass - Violinist. The location of the picture is listed as Douglas and Alabo Streets- 9ᵗʰ Ward. The band was looking very dapper in derbies sitting on chairs in someone's back yard with two unnamed children. The musicians are stylishly dressed in suits with hats. It would have stood to reason that a musician, who went to the countryside to help others set up a band, would surely set up his own band…. Several pictures were distributed in the same condition, the same as in the Family Tree Album. There is a print made from a broken glass pate negative which is part of the New Orleans Jazz Club collection at the Old mint, part of the far-flung Louisiana State Museum and is accompanied with two documents, one of which states the photo was given to trumpeter Herbert Morand by Willie Parker on November 7, 1948.Given for public use by Ms. Armontine palao and Mrs Andre Nuenutt distribution 1902 Family album >>

Around the corner from the Odd Fellows Hall, at Perdio and Rampart there was a regular "gin barbershop" where musicians were accustomed to hanging out while waiting to get calls for jobs. Palao got many gigs from there and he played for dances, parades, parties, with flexible personnel according to the nature of the job.

One day out on the lake, Jimmy said, he heard sounds from a cornet that he had never heard before. He was mesmerized, he rushed down the road and through the crowded area only to see Buddy Bolden playing, After, the performance Buddy rushed down to him and asked him to join his band. He thought about it for the next days. Buddy had natural talent and he learned so quickly. Buddy and his instrument were almost like glue, he played it almost 24-7. He took very little time for sleep. Jimmy always had such high hopes for Buddy and he had most definitely by passed all expectations. In 4 years Buddy had mastered the instrument and had won every contest/battle. He was known to New Orleanians as the "King of the cornet". Jimmy found it was becoming a hassle rounding up band members for open gigs. His band members didn't seem to be as devoted to the ragtime music. So Jimmy officially closed down this band, the only band that carried his name.(2)

Jimmie then joined the Buddy Bolden Band in-between 1903 and 1905. He was very impressed with the style of the music Buddy played. Even though Jimmy Palao taught Buddy how to read music and work with his instrument, the teacher now began to learn from the student. This was the music that Jimmy Palao would carry to national fame. Buddy Bolden wrote a little song, "The Old Crow Died" and "The Old Brock Cried" On this number the entire band which included Jimmy Palao sang the vocal chorus and they could really harmonize.

It was said that when it was time to start the dance, Buddy would holler, "Let's call the children home," and he'd put his horn out the window and blow, and everyone would come running. The talk about Buddy Bolden was how, on some nights, you could hear his horn ten miles away.(3) It very well could have happened, because the city of New Orleans has a different kind of acoustics from other cities. There is water all around the city. There is also water all under the city, which is one of the reasons why they would bury people above ground – in tombs, mounds, et cetera If you dug over three feet deep, you would come up with water. Adding to this dampness, there was the heat and humidity of the swamps, of the bayous all around New Orleans. From the meeting of the dampness and the heat, a mist, a vapor comes up into the air there, and there are continuously changing air currents. There also were no tall buildings in the early 1900's to block the air waves and the electrical currents cause very little blockage to sound. Sound travels better across water, and because of all those moving air currents, when you blew your horn in New Orleans – especially on a clear night – when guys like Bolden would blow their beautiful brass trumpets, the sound could carry more than 15 miles.(4) Unfortunately the talented Buddy Bolden had bouts of depression and he would just walk off the stage in the middle of a performance. His erratic behavior was causing trouble with band personnel. In 1905 Jimmy decided to leave Buddy's band. In 1907 Buddy was playing at a parade, they say he walked away and never played again.(5)

1903 James Palao holding cornet

Jimmy Palao loved to hear the musicians play so in 1906 he moved on to the Imperial Band and took leadership. He began developing the style of music he had come to love; he decided to feature each artist and to improvise upon with his best tune. This was what made Jazz...Jazz. It is believed that Jimmy was the first to coin this musical style. as Jazz as first evidenced on his business card with the earliest date of 1908 which is the first reference to the of style music that Buddy Bolden originated as ...Jaz, Jaz, Jaz Jimmy Palao felt the need to express his Jazz voice through his main instrument the violin. Through the years he became an accomplished and expressive Jazz violinist, earning a reputation as one of the finest Jazz violinists of his generation.

According to historical accounts in the early 1900's the leader of the Jazz band usually was a skilled and well trained violinist.(6) Jimmy Palao used the violin as a lead instrument to play in the higher positions, the notes could be heard above all the other instruments and could fall into almost any key (particularly the flat keys, beloved of wind players), and this method added a rich tone, particularly on slow numbers and allowed others who couldn't read music to follow and not get lost as they improvised upon the tune... Jimmy found that the key of B^b was comparable to all of the instruments especially the horns that were built in this key. So he arranged and transposed all of the music in the key of B^b. The key of B^b became the standard key for playing Jazz.(7) The violin was one of the key ingredients in classical music. It may be hard to imagine a violin in a Jazz band. The sound from the violin added a special flavor of horn-like phrasing to this new music, which was sometimes understandably, referred to as 'Classic Jazz'. For the violin player, Jazz has several challenging aspects which set it apart from most folk styles. Each number in a Jazz performance starts and ends with a melody which is played more or less "straight" (as written). The largest part of the composition is made up of improvised solos. This was the beginning of collective improvisation allowing every soloist to express and develop his own individual ideas and adding to the tune as a whole. (7)

The Imperial Orchestra under the leadership of Jimmy Palao was in demand and they were called on more and more to play this new style of music!

Jimmy Palao associated with some of the best and naturally talented Jazzmen in New Orleans. The chapters ahead will give evidence to his long career, He played with the following top Orchestra and Bands* in 1897 through 1922:

Buddy Johnson Band [Palao, Leader.] [1895-1897] **Manuel Manetta Interview, WR Collections** – Sacred Heart Of St MaryHall on Valiette at Eveline Street

Pacific Brass Band [1897-1898] – **Bocage Interview, WR Collection**

Henry Allen Brass Band [1897-1900 (picture)] **Jazzmen**

Jimmy Palao Band [Palao, Leader] [1900 (picture)]

Buddy Bolden Band [1903-1905

Imperial Jazz Band, [Palao, Leader] [1905-1907 (picture)] **Family Album** [Palao, Leader [1905 (picture)] **Singleton Family Album**

Olympia Band [1909]

Original Creole Orchestra[Palao, Leader] [1908] Town Topics Show [New Orleans, California, New York, NY, Chicago] [[1911-1915 (picture)] Alexander Pantage Tour, six month tour, August 11, 1914 [Washington, Oregon, Canada, Los Angeles, San Francisco, Oakland, San Diego] **Singleton Family Album**

Lawrence Duhe Band[1918-1919 (picture)] **Chicago Defender Jolly Jazzing Jeopards** [1921- Dreamland Cafe] **Family Album** There is a better copy of this picture in the **University of Chicago, John Steiner Collection**

King Joe Oliver Band [1919-1921 (picture)] **Jazzmen**

John Wickliffe's–Ginger Band [1922 (picture) **Sankofa Our Family Album**

Syncopated Gingersnaps [1922 (picture)**Family Tree Album**(2)]

Dave and Tessie Band [1922-1922 (picture)]

*All pictures published and distributed between 1909-1922..

Chapter Four

Jimmy Palao Played with Top Bands

Jimmy Palao Played with the following Jazz Artist:

Henry Allen - all brass
Louis Armstrong – sax
George Baquet – clarinet

Rene Baptiste - guitar
"Zino" Baltimore – drums
Peter Bocage – trombone
Buddy Bolden - cornet
Wellman Braud – bass
Jack Carey – trombone
"Mutt" Carey- trumpet
"Papa" Celestine – trumpet
Wallace Collins - trumpet
Eddie Dawson–guitar, bass
"Big Eye Delille – Clarinet
Frankie Dusen - trombone
Honore Dutrey – trombone
Sam Dutrey – clarinet

Dink Johnson – drums
Buddy Johnson - bandleader
William "Bill" Manuel Johnson
 – bass
Davey Jones – alto sax
Freddie Keppard –cornet
Porter Lamont - clarinet
Frank Lewis- guitar
Bob Lyons – bass
John MacMurray - drums
Manuel Manetta – all brass
Billy Marrero - bass
Bebe Mitchell - bass, tuba
Brock Mumford – guitar
Jimmie Noone – clarinet
Joe Oliver – trumpet
Roy Palmer – trombone
Manuel Perez – cornet

Lawrence Duhe – clarinet

George Field – trumpet

George Filhe - trombone

Gilbert "Babs"Frank - piccolo

George [Pops] Foster– bass

Charlie Galloway

"Montudi" Garland – bass

Vic Garpard - cornet

Albert Glenny - bass

Minor Hall – drums

Tubby Hall – drums

Lil Hardin – piano

George Hooker - cornet

Sugar Johnny – cornet

A.J. Piron – violin

Josh Portefield - bass

August Rousseau

Emmett Scott – banjo

Anthony Spaulding - sax

Johnny St. Cyr – banjo, guitar

Cornelius Tillman - drums

John Underwood - sax

Eddie Vincent – trombone

Ed Williams - banjo

Stanley "Fess" Williams - saxophone

Leon Williams – guitar

Norwood Williams – guitar

A photo of the Imperial Band dated 1905 shows violinist Jimmy Palao with leader on his cap while Rene Baptiste's cap has embroidered on it "MGR". This photograph serves as (Rose and Souchon 1967, 164) that James Palao was the leader of the Imperial Band in 1905 Band: his cap bears that legend.

1905 The Imperial Band Left to right; John MacMurray - Drums, George Filhe - Trombone, James A. Palao - Violin, "Big Eyed" Louis Nelson Delisle - Clarinet, Rene Baptiste - Guitar, Manuel Perez - Trumpet, Jimmy Brown - Bass Violin

The Imperial Band was formed in 1900. They played a mixture of blues, ragtime and traditional dance music. In 1905, Jimmy Palao took leadership of The Imperial Orchestra. Under his leadership they went from uniforms to tailored suits. A photo of the Imperial Orchestra dated 1905 shows the band in uniform, violinist Jimmy Palao with "leader" on his cap, while guitarist Rene Baptiste's cap has on it manager. Peter Bocage's interview also confirmed that Jimmy was the leader of the Imperial Orchestra In 1905. Jimmy began to individually work with the band members of the Imperial Orchestra on the tunes that they played the best. He then would allow that band member to star. The people loved the improvisations; they couldn't stop moving, they would twirl, twist, kick high and shake their moving feet and bodies as these musicians took their instruments to the highest and lowest listening level. This was becoming the music that people couldn't get enough of and the group was in high demand to be heard.(1)

It is documented in several books and interviews that Jimmy Palao played with Bill and Dink Johnson in various bands... Jimmy Palao was the leader and Bill Johnson was one of the co-managers in 1905 of the Imperial Band and this is obviously when the first bonds of friendship formed between

Johnson and Palao.(2) A relationship that brought the music Jimmy Palao called "Jazz" to the people. A relationship that lasted to Jimmy Palao's last days. A style of music that has lasted over 100 years is now heard coast to coast. In the years before the First World War, Jimmy Palao's Imperial Band was in constant demand for parades, dances, numerous picnics and outings. During this period he occasionally doubled on cello. In 1905, the Imperial Band and the band members were Buddy Johnson- trombone, "Big Eye Louis" Nelson-Clarinet, Rene Baptiste- guitar and Billy Marrero - bass. They are pictured playing on the Lake Pontchartrain. Much of what was called Milneburg early in the first third of this century was actually near Lake Pontchartrain... The buildings and dock walkways connecting them were on wooden pilings in the shallows of the lake. Downtown was very much different in those early years. There were many functions, especially downtown balls and parties — people liked to dance and have a good time, and there was always somewhere for the musicians to perform. They played in open stands near Lake Pontchartrain or at the pavilions out on the water. Every Sunday each group that gathered would hire a band of some sort. Lucian's Pavilion was on a platform out on the water, and Little Alice's Camp on the land. To get out to the lake front there were two narrow gauge steam trains. One ran out Bienville to the Spanish Fort, the other ran out Elysian Fields to Milneburg. They did not go fast, and you could easily run and jump on or off. Everybody rode out on Sunday to the picnics this way. The fare was 15 cents round trip. Some would walk out there, but it was about 3 or 4 miles. Others might hire a wagon for a group.

There was plenty of music and dancing at the lake every Sunday and weekend in the summer. The picnics at the lake were the ideal place for the younger people to hear the different bands and musicians. There would be seven or eight bands, as well as some smaller combos. They could be heard at the different camps and picnic grounds, and needless to say, the Imperial Orchestra drew the biggest crowd.

Jimmy Palao and the Imperial Band performed all over the city and at every gig available to them. They probably played a mixture of Jazz blues, ragtime and dance music. While on the road they were faced with rough traveling conditions. Johnny St. Cyr said "I can remember about this time they would use furniture wagons, drawn by horses, with a band riding on the wagon playing from, say, Claiborne and Dumaine to Rampart and back to Galvez. They would cover a whole area, approximately a six mile radius. For example in the Creole section they would cover both open ends of the area in two days. In later years, when using trucks to carry the musicians they would cover the entire area or whole city in a day."(3)

In the very early days the bands played for subscription parties. New Orleanians never lost their penchant for dancing, and most of the city's brass band members doubled as dance band players. You subscribed to a party (allowed to buy a ticket or tickets) and only ticket holders were admitted. This was the way in which they kept out the riff-raff or other problems. The bands played for birthday parties, weddings, anniversaries and celebrations of all kinds. Around 1900 Orleans Street, near the Treme Public Market or in the centre of the street, all of the fans could see the musicians entering the clubs or homes and everyone knew them all.. They were a musical inspiration for the young and old.

In 1905 Jimmy met and married. Armontine Carter a 19 year old maiden Armontine married James "Jimmy' Palao on October 3, 1905 at St Catherine's Church, New Orleans, Louisiana.(4) Armontine was a native of Barbados and had immigrated to New Orleans when she was five or six years old. She recalled that her grandmother was from Haiti. Her father was from Cuba and he spoke Spanish. Armontine spoke French and Spanish fluently. She was considered a Barbadian, they call themselves Bajans.

1905 - Imperial Band;:John Mac Murray - Drums, George Filhe - Trombone, Manuel Perez - Trumpet, Big Eye Louis" Nelson - Clarinet, James A. Palao, Leader and Violinist, Rene Baptiste - Guitar, Jimmy Brown - Bass Violin Well dressed in suits with hats Picture taken October 25, 1905, Union Station Park, New Orleans Public distribution 1905, New Orleans, Louisiana. Photographer A. Zeringue died 1920.

Armontine remembered meeting "Jimmy" at the first dance she ever attended at Violet Hall presumably in the small community of Violet in St Bernard Parish, three miles downriver from Chalmette. The music was performed by the Imperial Orchestra of which Jimmy was the leader. Armontine said all of the men were good looking and well dressed in suits. Each time Armontine told the story she would smile and heartily laugh. A very youthful look would go across her face as she would take you back to the time she and Jimmy Palao first saw one another... She said "Jimmy was playing on stage and she could barely take her eyes off of him. He glanced at her and in that moment their eyes locked. He was so taken with her he could barely concentrate. He had one of the musicians from the band go over to her and ask her for the dance with him during his first break. She responded saying she couldn't because she didn't know how to dance. He then sent another fellow over, who said he would teach her. The music began slowly and the young man took her on the floor and they began to dance step by step. He told her she was a natural dancer.

Then Jimmy Palao took a break and the band continued to play." It seems as though time stands still or is frozen in your memory when you meet the love of your life. Your heart sets it sights on that individual it doesn't consult with your mind... nothing else exist. It is as though there is no one else but the two of you in the universe. She said he introduced himself smiled and asked her to dance. He took her in his arms and said "Just follow me" they glided across the floor and Armontine said she fell in love with him that very moment. They talked for over an hour. He said he didn't work two days of the week. So thereafter, every Tuesday and Thursday he would pick her up from her home and they would go to the Hall and dance and talk endlessly. She said he was quite a dancer and light on his feet, she followed his steps with ease. A few of his musicians friends later revealed that Jimmy never took days off until he met Armontine. She had heard from a few of the town's people that he was a womanizer, a charmer, a real ladies man, in love with all women and never true to one. She knew she would be a fool to think she could have a meaningful relationship with him. He was handsome, charismatic and probably just as incapable of fidelity. He had wavy silky hair, chiseled keen features, his clothes were the finest and the scent of his cologne was overwhelming. She took note of the women who always hung around, but he only looked at her. One evening he asked to marry her and of course without hesitation… she said yes.

They had a small wedding with their family and friends present… George Hooker one of his childhood buddies who had played cornet in the Pacific Brass Band with him, stood as witness to the ceremony. Armontine had yards of the finest handmade lace given to her many a year before by her mother. She was a seamstress and she worked day and night on her dress it was beautiful the lace laid softly amongst the pearl and crystal beading on a backing of silk. She said, he never took his eyes off of her during the entire ceremony. He trembled a little and she firmly steadied his hand and he smiled. Felix Palao gave them a Family Bible which Armontine treasured her entire life. After marriage Jimmy and Armontine lived only briefly in the Spriggs house in Algiers… Their first baby was born crippled and he was 4 months old, in 1906 when he died. Armontine thought that Jimmy already had one child named Joe when they were married. The mother was a lady of the evening and had unscrupulous ties with the underworld. His name was Joe Palao and he was later recalled by Tom Albert as a long time employee of Blandin's Funeral Home. He said Joe had worked at this funeral home since he was a boy. It was said that Joe played the trumpet and he lived on St. Peter Street in New Orleans. Jimmy never mentioned the birth or existence of this child and he always avoided the subject. Armontine never saw Joe Palao and to her knowledge he never had a relationship with Jimmy. Armontine later learned Joe Palao wasn't Jimmy's child but carried the last name, Palao to protect the father's identity.

In Jimmy's younger days he didn't have… or perhaps I should say he didn't take the time to form a meaningful relationship with females. During these years there were a number of woman in and out of his life. Armontine said Jimmy revealed to her he was frightened of becoming too close to a woman for fear she would bear a son and die as had his Grandmother and Mother. She said some voodoo woman had told him he was cursed. Armontine was a woman of strong faith and she convinced him this was utter nonsense. He apparently took her at her word because the subject never came up again

Armontine often mentioned how beautifully Jimmy played the violin. She said he could make incredible tones come from that violin and the sounds were unbelievable, they were so full and clear. According to Armontine she said Jimmy found that when using fast strokes he could reach a wide array of notes and harmonic tones or when he played different octaves he could achieve a full, rich sound. He once wrote a tune especially for her and he played the saxophone with such deep feelings it would bring tears to her eyes. She said he really knew how to play every instrument in the band. Armontine said Eddie Vincent told her that Jimmy had taught him and Buddy Bolden how to read music. She said that Jimmy from the very first time he met her in 1905, he referred to the music he played as "Jazz". She said he talked a lot to her about the music, the musicians and the gigs they played. He was always playing one instrument or another. Sometimes he would go into the back room of their apartment and would play until it was time to meet with the band members. Armontine said she would have to remind him to eat before he would leave. I also must mention that Armontine could cook like the best chef on earth. Her food was extremely flavorful; she was an artist in the kitchen. I even miss those aromas from her kitchen She was affectionately nicknamed "Cookie"(5)

Jimmy Palao continued as leader with the Imperial Orchestra in 1906 was active in the district and was becoming very popular, especially at 101 Ranch and the 138 Villa Cabaret, in New Orleans. They also played in the played in the local bordello's, the dives, the joints and what was known in the neighborhood as "the bucket of blood saloons" Jonathan Finkelman, musician, says "From what I understand, there used to be gun fights in there and knife fights and at the end of the night when they were cleaning up, they used to pour out a "bucket of blood,"(6)

1905, Milneburg Picnic Buddy Johnson - trombone, Big eyed Louis nelson Delille - clarinet, Jimmy Palao - violin; Rene Baptize - Guitar; Billy Marrero - bass: Note: The musicians are dressed in suits with hats Picture cropped

Jimmy stayed away from the minstrel shows, they almost seemed degrading and he found no humor in the Blackface images. He rather play in the joints of New Orleans than to be laughed at. They played in homes for entertainment; there were many playing opportunities in the bars and clubs that dotted 'Storyville' and the adjacent areas.

1905 – Milneburg Picnic Buddy Johnson - trombone, Big eyed Louis Nelson Delille - clarinet, Jimmy Palao - violin; Rene baptize - Guitar; Billy Marrero - bass:

Sidney Story, the Mayor of New Orleans plan wasn't to legalize prostitution and crime but to control it. . In 1887 there was an attempt to keep vice in a 28 block restricted area just below Canal street. This was 'Storyville' known as the District. In 1889 this area became the officially legal unique red-light district, the only one in the U.S. established by law. Storyville's brothels, sporting houses, and saloons, dives and cabarets flourished. The concept worked for nearly two decades and ironically the District became one of the City's leading tourist attractions. Their activities demanded musical accompaniment and their customers bankrolled every moment of it. They came from everywhere. Storyville was a rough area; the streets were lined with "bars and cribs" tiny rooms for prostitutes, fancy brothels, in which prostitution was tolerated (for whites only). Ladies of the evening advertised in store front windows, drug use was wide spread, gambling where men lost their pay checks, many were turned out on the street penniless. Many were unable to return to the cities or states they had come from. Patrons and police carried guns to settle frequent fights. Many were left to roam the streets as vagabonds. It was in Storyville, with the parades on the streets, on the riverboat that resting and moved on the waters that carried the beginning small currents of the music we now call Jazz. Al Rose calculated that Storyville provided work for over 12 thousand people and about 50 musicians on an average night. Elaborate bordellos, fancy restaurants and dance halls quickly appeared and flourished, along Basin, the street that was to become a legend because of its later association with early Jazz.

The dark spiritual haunted side of New Orleans is compelling as the eerie stories about real people, murdered victims and sightings of ghost and the sounds of strange music in the background. It has often been said that only in New Orleans could darkness be so intriguing! The Bordello Mansion paid homage to the wanton pleasures that were once known in 'Storyville'. Preserved in its original style as described in the Creole Garden brochure each room was decorated in a different shade of red and is named after a famous New Orleans Madame of the time. Each room features deluxe queen sized canopy or four poster beds, (one room has king size), hardwood floors, high ceilings, hand sewn bedding and drapes and beau coups eccentric everywhere, turn-of-the-century decadence and debauchery New Orleans style! The madams of these brothels would hire mainly Creole musicians to entertain their clients in the saloons and brothel houses. Here many musicians found their niche. Without very critical audiences, these musicians were given a great deal of freedom with the ladies of the evening.

As far as the District was concerned Armontine never went down there to hear Jimmy play. It wasn't a place for a respectable woman to be seen. She once said "There was so much crime and violence I was afraid to go there. Even though I have ridden through the area on the Villare Streetcar but I never stopped there. I would have been afraid to. Besides Jimmy didn't want me there I once saw a group of rough, tough looking ladies walking into one of the big houses along the row and I wondered if they were prostitutes.". 'Storyville' was near a train station and many visitors to the city also frequented the bordellos and the clubs to listen to and dance to this new music.

The description that Al Rose gives in his book Storyville... The first of the districts of New Orleans to attain special notoriety in 1820 was the "Swamp," an area bounded by South Liberty and South Robertson streets, and by Girod and Julia streets.... Murders were plentiful; the Police dared not enter this area, unless they were in groups. Many men were missing who were caught in the "Swamp", drugged, beaten and with no money. They had either gambled it away or were lured in by prostitutes. It was called "the port of missing men" This area was closed down in 1870. In 1870 the prostitutes were crowded into "Smoky Row" a single block of Burgundy Street between Conti and Bienville streets, prostitutes openly flaunted sex. The half naked women sat in rocking chairs or on the curbs. I thoroughly agree with Al Rose who said "Jazz did not start in "Storyville", the "Swamp" or in "Smoky Row", nor was it reared there. Jimmy Palao once in his early teens went to "Smoky Row". These small sections of New Orleans were havens of vice and sin. "Smoky Row" was dismantled by the police in 1887.(7)

Jimmie Palao on the Riverboat on the Mississippi. The picture above which was taken in early 1908 suggest that Jimmy Palao did a gig on the steamboat before forming the Original Creole Band.

Most of New Orleanians had a sophisticated air. A fundamental attribute of New Orleans was the perennial party atmosphere. This was also melting pot of a lot of clean fun. New Orleans was a cosmopolitan amusement park. Thus music was always in demand, not just as paid entertainment but as the soundtrack of a never-ending party. There were brass bands Caucasians, Creole's and African American's that marched in parades as they strutted in the hot sunlight. One might see bands riding to town on trucks to advertise a dance or event. During the daylight hours the funeral processions were among the most colorful memories marching out to the cemeteries.

The men who played by day were for the most part the same men who worked in the joints of the district by night. All carving their way to the most serious musical art form created in America. Jimmy Palao never forgot the sounds created by improvisation when these musicians let loose He carried what he had learned in 1903 from Buddy Bolden's Band into his future travels and as developed this style of music it would later revolutionize the culture around him.(8)

Jimmy Palao played with all of the top musicians of the day in the clubs, on the streets of New Orleans and on the River. From the interview with Josh Portefield trombonist he said "When Jimmy Palao played with these musicians in the back room and to those outside listening, it was an incredible thing. If you had been there, you would have seen it was a very disorganized and unbalanced scene yet. Jimmy Palao would pull the musicians together. Then the music would hit your inner soul like a bolt of lightning. In that field of leader of the band, he was the last word. He was a musical genius, ahead of his time and. everybody dug him and those cats played very hard for him night after night…"

Then one night, Jimmy Palao was listening to the public battles, he heard Keppard, who sounded so good it made everyone dizzy. Jimmy Palao and Keppard became running buddies and William Johnson joined the Imperial Orchestra. Under the leadership of Jimmy Palao, William Johnson executed big bass sounds as he strummed the strings and rhythmically slapped the double bass. He would suddenly twirl the bass around on its end pin and he never missed a beat or note. Johnson was credited with being the first to perform this style of playing the double bass. George Baquet, a good friend of Jimmy's and he was a extremely talented musician. Jimmy was so taken with the sweet sounds that Baquet eschewed from his horn that he dedicated a composition he wrote called "O You Sweet Rag" to George Baquet.

There was just a handful of fine violinist and Jimmy was one of the best. He loved classics. He never lost his passion and desire to play good music. He presented Jazz from its beginnings as a serious and sophisticated music. The Jazz musicians he played with were well rehearsed, in reading and playing special stock arrangements

Jimmy Palao and Freddie Keppard

I have searched for and found a few of the black faced characterizations by few white reviewers. I did not find a lot of evidence of this from those who attended the Jazz events. There were a few reviewers from the white media who had a lot of difficulty taking this new music seriously. Jazz wasn't a minstrel show nor was it just a dancing music it was also a listening music and it showcased professionally talented musicians. Unfortunately some historians seem to delight in carrying the bigoted views that presents only these few cartoon drawings which stuck to the old stereotypes and black face characterizations. Most ads describing the Jazz dance bands were of positive and of well dressed musicians. However as a result of more and more whites beginning to appear as an interested audience. The little petty minded interviewer's stereo types were disappearing. The Jazz music that Americans were enjoying and tapping a beat to and dancing to, this music they couldn't get enough of was… taking hold.(9) The audiences grew larger and larger. Their performances were sold out to standing crowds only. What a joy!

The Original Creole Orchestra always received separate billing. They were a real class act of professional musicians. Vaudeville acts were made up of a series of separate, unrelated acts grouped together on a common bill. On occasion as part of the vaudeville circuit, their act was followed by a comedian in Black face singing Old Black Joe. H. Prince Morgan's, role was dual he would appear in blackface and then he would come on stage as this well dressed singer and dancer. No act of this nature ever appeared on stage with them when they played off circuit. Leonard Scott who is mentioned in a later chapter as a singer and comedian apparently was on the Vaudeville bill after Prince took ill. Let it be understood that at no time was the band ever in blackface makeup. They were billed separate by Bill Johnson who managed the band. The minstrel shows that were originally performed by African-Americans were a celebration of African-American music and dance. It is when whites began to dress up in tattered clothing and began rubbing burnt cork on their face that the shows eventually became offensive.(10)

Jimmy Palao was a good musician, a real heavy (slang) and he influenced many notable musicians and bands from diverse genres. Someone many a year ago posed the following scenario. How often do you ever see someone who is really together in image and in head? The music fits in with the person, the person fits in with the musicians and all became one... Thus begins the story of the Original Creole Orchestra in 1908... Jimmy Palao led the Original Creole Orchestra on its remarkable journey of a lifetime beginning in 1908, from New Orleans, to California, to Chicago, to New York and. to cities throughout the USA and Canada

Yet what amazes me the most is that even today whenever I have mentioned the names of Jimmy Palao, Freddie Keppard or Buddy Bolden they are immediately recognized.

Chapter Five

First to Coin Term "Jaz"
The Original Creole Band 1908

The origin of the word "Jazz" is one of the most sought-after word origins in modern American English. False assumptions and incorrect information from even the most respected sources have led to widespread confusion as to the word's history. Nevertheless, the word's intrinsic interest — the American Dialect Society named it the Word of the Twentieth Century which has resulted in considerable research.(1) Sometimes answers are hard to realize ... "Because people spend years looking for deep and complicated answers or hidden messages. I guess a complicated answer would make the subject a lot more interesting.

Some years ago, when I tried to sort through the deeper motivations of someone close to me, I was told that "I'm really not that deep or complicated. What you see is what you get. I keep it real." We may never truthfully know what brought about or motivated the use of the word Jazz, only one man whom was believed to be the originator, Jimmy Palao knows that and the secret died with him. However, there is no denying what we see. So I began to search for the way to find the answer. Its strange how we overlook what's right under our nose. One day while looking through the family album I found the earliest reference to the word, or evidence of the first written musical term Jaz, Jas. Jazz, or Jass and there it was where it had always been in records and books, the 1908, 1911 and 1914 business cards of Jimmy Palao.

Al Rose provided this business card dated on the back 1908 to Clotilde Palao-Wilson

It is believed that Jimmy Palao started using the term Jazz in 1905 when he played with the Imperial Band. There is also a record of James Palao's 1908 business card which was provided by Al Rose to Clotilde Wilson, when she met with him in Florida. This was the most tangible and first physical and direct evidence that provides an answer to the question of when and who coined the musical term "Jaz". This was the first time the term "Jaz" appeared in print.(2) All of this information adds to the evidence that James Palao as leader of the Original Creole Orchestra was the first to use the word "Jaz" to describe the music that comes from New Orleans. The double zz was added later. (Jazz) The historical circumstances paint a picture that leads to the same conclusion: that James "Jimmy" Palao was the first to coin the musical term Jazz. The term "Jazz" became a traveling word and any time the term was mentioned or referenced to in these early years, after thorough research it became clear, that it was no coincidence that the musical term was always used when James Palao was around or nearby. Even the account is true that the term "Jazz" was first mentioned in 1914 in California and Chicago. James certainly was in California and Chicago in 1914 as evidenced by his itinerary and business card of 1914. It seems from all accounts that James Palao had the best opportunity to spread the term "Jazz' by word of mouth and through distributing his business cards because as of record he was in or associated with most of the major Jazz bands from New Orleans. At some point he came in direct contact with most of the unknown and well known Jazz musicians.

Jimmy Palao's wife Armontine said he always referred to the music he played as "Jazz." from the time she met him in 1905.(3) The word

'Jazz' has become a part of American culture. In its original connotation, "Jaz" or "Jas" or if simple reasoning is more acceptable it could have been on the card he named this style of music after himself, (James) and he called the music he played "Jaz" or "Jas". Although he shows no desire to be recognized separate and apart from his band members in anything we have heard about him. Yet, it is not too difficult to believe he would name the music he so loved to share under his name. I can expound upon the fact that: "If one is to ever understand Jazz as an intelligent serious and complex art form they will also understand that the musical arts carry no hidden connotations or meanings. Jazz is the most free and pure art form that exists. One must remember that the arts are an emotion, a truth they tell a story, they tell it like it is and they keep it real. With Jazz everything is out in the open and everything is new and nothing is hidden. There is no tune played the same. If we must seek answers and find facts concerning this great art form created in America, let the reasoning be based upon the higher scale that "Jazz" has achieved. These men were educated and professional Jazzmen who respected the music they played. James Palao was very thorough in his presentation of Jazz as a serious art form. He insisted the band members rehearse night and day, before and after performances. He was driven. It certainly comes as no surprise and it is logical, that a man who was so concerned with every detail of developing this different musical style, would certainly be the one to give name to the music he played….

From what we can gather from Pops Foster interview was that Bill Johnson left the Imperial band because he wanted to have full say so and manage his own band. As a co-manager he couldn't get Rene Baptiste to book outside of New Orleans.(4) It was said Rene seemed a little fearful of traveling. I was unable to find out what happened to Rene Baptiste after he left the Imperial Band. There is no record that I could find of Rene traveling and or playing with any other bands. In Jean Christopher Averty's notes bassist Bill Johnson set up a band in with a cornet player, Ernest Coycault and a trombonist, Albert Paddio. (5) In 1906 Bill Johnson was in New Orleans when he heard about the earthquake in San Francisco. One of the areas that were almost completely destroyed in the 1906 disaster was the "Barbary Coast". There was nothing left but a den of waterfront depravity that loosely stretched from the famed Embarcadero to the Presido - a sprawling 40 ft square block. Nearly all of the drinking and dancing establishments on the Barbary Coast were erased in the aftershock from the fires that followed the devastating 1906 earthquake. Within months a dozen or so of those establishments were rebuilt and back in business. Bill Johnson saw this as a business opportunity for the band so he returned to California and around 1907. He opened a cigar store and pool parlor in Oakland. At a later date Johnson opened another poolroom in Los Angeles which his mother and sister Bessie operated. Johnson took to the road and began to arrange most of his business deals.(6)

In 1907 Johnson, Ernest Coycault (trumpeter) and Albert Paddio (trombonist) left New Orleans by train to go to Los Angeles. More substantiation of the California tour came from Benjamin "Reb" Spikes, [a musician] who is reported as saying: "There wasn't much music in Los Angeles I remember before I went to Frisco in 1907. Will Johnson came here in 1907, playing' bass with his Creole Band. He and Ernest Coycault who called himself Johnson's sibling... because Will and he looked so much alike everybody thought they were brothers. Bill found Los Angeles had the right climate for his business venture. They organized a "get-up" band that in 1908 and took the train to California, stopping along the way at such towns as Houston, Dallas, Waco, and Yuma. This band consisted of William Johnson, mandolin; Alphonse Ferzand, bass (said now to have been from Biloxi); Paddio, valve trombone; Charles Washington, guitar; and Ernest Coycault; trumpet. The group played for a month at the Red Feather tavern in Los Angeles, but they did not go to San Francisco and they didn't return to New Orleans with Johnson.

Bill Johnson then set up a Creole band in New Orleans which included. William Toncel, mandolin; Bill Johnson, guitar; Alphonse Ferzand, bass; Charley "Henderson" (the quotation marks are in Averty's notes), banjo; John Collins, trumpet. Apparently they were asked to travel to Chicago and New York, but no one wanted to leave New Orleans.

The group broke up. Research is very sketchy during these beginning years. There is a spotted recall of the gigs they played. The chief documentation of their performances came from the mainstream white theatrical press and the media and they did not work the black vaudeville circuits. There were only few articles that made any reference to their performances. The group received some mention in the local general newspapers that were drawn from a few press releases. The search for dramatically symbolic landmarks that can make sense out of the early history of Jazz is perhaps not conducive to answering relevant questions. The participants in events may show favor to their own interpretations in their recollections. Something of this sort appears to have occurred in the process of gathering information that began with Bill Russell's research for Jazzmen in 1938. Bill needed an experienced band leader and he recalled how well he and Jimmy had worked together with the Imperial Band. He also remembered how excited the audience would get when that band would play. Bill had not been able to execute that "New Orleans syncopated beat", that Jimmy called "Jazz", with any of the bands he formed Bill Johnson had been unable to locate Jimmy Palao to arrange a meeting with him. It seemed that Jimmy was always on the road. Johnson returned to New Orleans and one day passing through the French Quarter he saw Jimmy Palao and they greeted each other as old friends do and they sat down and talked for hours… Bill Johnson, a few days later met again with Jimmy Palao…

According to historical accounts in late 1908 James Palao and Bill Johnson formed a firm partnership. What a match! The best professional director and most versatile musician, Jimmy Palao, joined forces with Bill Johnson, a gregarious and resourceful manager with considerable musical experience (he was forty years old already). Bill Johnson and Jimmy Palao founded and registered the Original Creole Orchestra in June 1908.(7) Jimmy began the process of selecting and inviting the best musicians from New Orleans, which he thought would fit into the Original Creole Orchestra. He put together a band of incredible musicians whose contrasting styles could result in meeting the end result he was looking for. He sought those with a repertoire of least four solos that he knew would get the audience off their feet. He chose these Jazzmen on the basis of talent and intellectual admiration, not on birthrights, even though they all were Creoles, Freddie Keppard - cornet, George Baquet -clarinet, Eddie Vincent - trombone, Danny Lewis – bass. Dink Johnson – drums.(8)

Setting up a band isn't an easy process, its more than just playing music together. It didn't happen overnight it required days and hours of practice and rehearsing, going over arrangements. The 1908 year, is readily confirmed by George Baquet's account that, "In 1908 the Original Creole Orchestra traveled on 'a hustlin' trip all over Dixie, making money as they barnstormed, just like the German bands used to do at that time'". Dink Johnson drums and Norwood Williams-guitar joined the group about 1909 on one of their trips to California.(8) These men were professionals and they were perfectionist. In between they played other gigs to keep their cash flow going. Playing syncopated music and improvising required skills which all of these gentlemen had perfected. They were ready and they shook the rafters and received standing ovations they were more than good. Their hard work and preparation time paid off.

Jimmy was seldom home with his family at this time. The band was confronted with racism on the Dixie tour. Unfortunately, during these years most Southern states had passed laws that created two separate societies: one Black, the other White. The combination of constant humiliation, dismal economic opportunities, of African Americans made traveling to the South by these Creole musicians very dangerous. Coming from New Orleans they were not accustom to such ill treatment. In most of the southern states, Blacks and whites could not ride together in the same railroad cars, sit in the same restaurants, or sit in the same theaters, drink from the same drinking fountain, swim in the swimming pool or use the same bathroom facilities. Blacks were denied access to parks, beaches, picnic areas, and from many hospitals. There was segregation in hotels, stores, and entertainment. In most instances the unsanitary conditions of the Black facilities were unworthy of any human being. In other words, these facilities were just plain nasty.(9)

Jimmy and Bill made the decision to not cross the Dixie line beyond New Orleans again with the Original Creole Orchestra. Little did they know the danger they had avoided, they later discovered that in some southern states there were Jim Crow laws to lynch and kill any one of mixed blood. I feel I have given enough information on the subject of racism to allow your imagination to take hold. I purposely at this point in my writings chose not to concentrate on this senselessness, because it seems as though these musicians were fortunate and encountered very little racism. Racism in America is a long story within itself and would create too much of a diversion from the story being told. Jazz was brought into being by a mixture and combination of cultures that represent the way of America life... and broke many racial barriers.

It can be said that you will seldom meet a Jazz musician who cares about the color of a person's skin. One of the greatest beauties of Jazz form its very beginnings is that it has the power to transcend race and gender.. Jazz is a great equalizer in this respect because one cannot fake the notion that one is a Jazz musician; if you cannot play Jazz, it becomes immediately apparent the moment you start to perform. The complexities of Jazz made it difficult for many to grasp and learn. Jazz musicians greatly admire and appreciate the sheer dedication of anyone who can learn how to perform the music well.

In summary Bassist Bill was known to be very convincing to those who were resistance to change and he had a reputation of getting the best gigs. He was a very good bassist and he did not play with the band until 1909 when Danny Lewis took ill. Johnson was also busy setting up performances. The band played many of the gigs he arranged in New Orleans. The first band to play the New York theaters was The Original Creole Orchestra by Jimmy Palao This band also opened in a show called the Town Topics at the Winter Garden Theatre

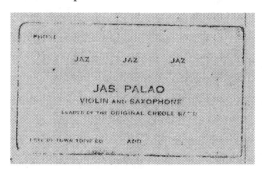

James Palao #2 Business card dated 1910. Played in Town Topic Show 1909

Bill Johnson continued to manage and book the gigs for the Original Creole Band in New York, Chicago and California. Palao would continue with the tours and stayed with the band. He never missed a performance and/or rehearsal. Johnson would go out scout the locations, arrange the bookings and set up the area for the band to play. There is also mention of Bill Johnson and Jimmy Palao performing in 1908 with the Original Creole Orchestra at the Los Angeles Dreamland at 8th and Spring St. They then played on the Barbary Coast in San

Francisco. It was at this point that they realized that the band member's incredible musical energy had captured the crowd as they roared for more. On their trip to California, Bill Johnson had warned them about the Barbary Coast even though the area now after rebuilding was a little safer. There were still vices all over the area. Jimmy and Bill after one gig in the cut throat atmosphere decided that this was not the place to advance the type of music they were playing. The Original Creole Orchestra returned to New Orleans. Jimmy arrived just in time for the birth of his first born daughter, Clotilde Palao. It was a joyous moment all of his family was there to celebrate. Bill Johnson went to Los Angeles in 1909 to organize his business base in California. He signed a contract with Town Topics which took the Original Creole Orchestra to New York, N.Y. to Chicago in 1909 to California back to New Orleans. They traveled extensively during this period. After each performance the audience would give them long standing ovations.(10) .

Poster as printed 1911 in Jazzmen and in Chicago Defender

The Original Creole Orchestra came to Chicago 1911 at the Grand Theater. Keppard and all there Bill Williams made a hit and brought on jealousy of the Northern brothers. Creole brothers down South heard of their success one by one to the land of the free and plenty dollars. Chicago Defender

The Original Creole Orchestra traveled to Los Angeles for a time and added a drummer Dink Johnson. (Brother of Bill Johnson). Around 1909 Danny Lewis was ailing and Bill Johnson took the bass position and went on to Chicago and played at the Grand Theater. In 1911 the Original Creole Orchestra was the first Jazz Orchestra to come to Chicago from New Orleans. This was the also the first time they played a theater with an almost exclusively African American patronage. (11) According to many accounts of Chicago and Jazz history, it was the arrival of this band with Jimmy Palao as leader that heralded the beginning of what would become an intense interest in Jazz and the impact was beginning to be felt.

The band returned to New Orleans and after arriving a month or two later on May 26, 1912, Jimmy's second daughter Mable Palao was born. The Palao, Spriggs and Carter family gathered again. Johnson then went to LA to set up gigs for the band. Los Angeles was becoming a major city and was growing by leaps and bounds. It was during this period that "Jazz" began to take shape in becoming a disciplined sophisticated art form. A few more of the musicians decided to test the water in Los Angeles and they boarded the trains on their way there. Los Angeles was considered the bourgeois capitol of the world. The Blacks were mostly affluent and formally educated and this was reflected in their musical training and they preferred to not associate with Blacks of the rural south. So it obviously was no coincidence that the Original Creole Orchestra and its musicians enjoyed the greater success in Los Angeles. Some people believed that Louisiana's Creole People (Creoles of Color) class system was built upon color or the hue of the skin. This distinction was made out of ignorance by people who knew no better. From what I can determine from parentage, all of the men in the Original Creole Band were Creole by birth. Louisiana has always been the Ancestral home for Creoles since the Foundation of the French Colony of Louisiana. .Creole Culture begun there and It flourished for over 200 years, but since the Civil War New Orleans, at one time the second largest City in America fell victim of the views of the South...

California has the largest population of Creole people outside the State of Louisiana. In Los Angeles, Creoles were known to be well educated and had excellent reading skills. The variations of New Orleans Jazz, was tough to play, the tempos were difficult and there were lots of key changes in improvisation. This made the music difficult for others to play; even those who could read music still couldn't mimic this Jazz style, which had been perfected specifically by this group of New Orleans Jazzmen.(12)

A review from the Times Picaynne, dated March 25,1913, read; "Here a Negro Band holds forth and from about 8 o'clock at night to 4 o'clock in the morning plays various rags, conspicuous for being the latest in popular music interspersed with compositions by the musicians themselves".. The driving syncopated style of New Orleans Jazz was beginning to transform the Jazz scene. It must be noted that the New Orleans musicians alone had mastered the professional reading abilities and learned skills of improvisation which rendered the professional survival of Jazz. This style of Jazz played by the Original Creole Orchestra was infectious, the audience would shout for more and some sessions would last almost an hour longer. The band members as tired as they were continued to play, they loved the response they were getting. This explains why one of Jimmy Palao's business card had Creole printed on it. It was a selling point, Creole musicians were in high demand in Los Angeles, Chicago, and New York because their ability to play New Orleans Jazz...

Jimmy Palao Business Card (Creole)

The Original Creole Orchestra returned to New Orleans. Then the inevitable occurred, Armontine separated from Jimmy Palao around October 1912, his various suspected escapades had taken a toll on the marriage. She had captured him in an undesirable moment. It wasn't a pretty scene. Armontine was heartbroken. She said they both cried. He wasn't a man to cry. She wasn't a woman to cry, but she cried night after night. She moved to a house with an old lady and stored all of her furniture in one room... A city directory listed Jimmy Palao at 2204 Annette St. (at about Miro St.). He continued to send her money to support her and his daughters. He kept calling her and she refused to see him. Jimmy had been on the road a lot, with the Original Creole Orchestra.

During the ten months that Jimmy was estranged from his wife 1912-1913, he was on the road most of the time. He was hurt by the breakup and longed for Armontine. He didn't slow down. He was scared to think, he even started drinking. He was seen with woman after woman. He became involved in New Orleans with one of Rene Baptiste distant cousins, Celestial Baptiste. Little is known about this particular moment in Jimmy's life. He according to his musician friends became more involved in his music and traveling with the band. At least that's what they told Armontine.(13)

New Orleans Clubs were popping: and the popular bands played in the Arlington Annex, the Cadillac, Frank Early's, 101 Ranch, the Frenchmen's, and Pete Lala's. The great musicians of New Orleans all played in the clubs and many doubled during the day or night. Jimmy occasionally subbed for Baquet at the 101 Ranch which was owned by Billy Phillips or he would fill in at the Tuxedo Club which was across the street and was owned by Harry Parker. Bill Russell also said, that all of the future great Jazz musicians could be seen at either one of these clubs. On April 13, 1913, Jimmy had just returned from Chicago and was called by Keppard to fill in for a gig at the Tuxedo Club. It was Easter Sunday morning about 3 AM, while Jimmy was playing on stage the owner of the 101 Ranch appeared with a bunch of New York thugs and opened gunfire leaving bodies all over the place. There was so much gunfire all you could see was smoke. Both owners of these cabarets were killed along with three of their men and surprisingly none of the musicians got killed. It was said that Manuel Manetta , Freddie

Keppard and Jimmy Palao all fell down to the floor and took refuge behind the piano. They crawled over to the back edge of the stage and climbed down a rope from the bandstand and then escaped through a trapdoor or backdoor behind the bandstand. Jimmy Palao never went back to play in Storyville again. He read the newspapers the next day. The newspapers called it the Easter Sunday Massacre, they said 40 people or more were wounded and died. For a moment he realized he could have died and would have never seen his wife, children and father again.(14)

Not long after that he went to Armontine and he pleaded with her to forgive him. He told her "For the first time in his life he was miserable". He swore he'd never hurt her again. He said he'd never set his foot in Storyville again. He told her of his plans to go to LA and he assured her he would change his ways and they could start afresh in California. He said he and the Original Creole Orchestra were in demand and he felt they were going to make it big. However, he said he wouldn't go to California without her and his children, (Clotilde and Mable). After a few months and many conversations and meetings with him, she called him and told him to meet her in California. She sold her furniture for $19 and used the $17 for a one way ticket to Los Angeles California. Little did she know that her decision to go to California was responsible for her husband's arrival and under his leadership, the Original Creole Orchestra and Jazz was about to take off..(15)

I would like to take this moment to correct an error in one of the writings of a Jazz historian concerning the work that Armontine did after arriving in Los Angeles. Bill Johnson offered her a job acting as a receptionist fronting for a lottery held in the back of the store. In the book it states she accepted this position. However we have her statement on tape, she refused his offer. Armontine was a Christian lady of undisputable class and virtue. She did acquire a job as a dressmaker once she arrived in Los Angeles. She was most definite in her rejection of the offer to work for Bill Johnson.(16) I make this correction with no disrespect for the work of this Jazz scholar who labored for years researching. the life of Jimmy Palao and the Original Creole Orchestra.

On Jimmy's way to Los Angeles it was said he woke up the entire train screaming and shouting. He had a bad dream and was clearly shaken. The next day as he got off the train an old lady selling rosaries walked up to him. She looked him directly in the eye for a moment and smiled and said "Don't look back!" Before he could answer, she said "Just don't look back! She then disappeared into the crowd. He took his bags and as he walked down the wooden railroad platform. He looked for the lady however, he didn't see her again. What was the vision he had seen in his dreams? No one knows what went through his thoughts, one can only imagine, but he never looked back.(17)

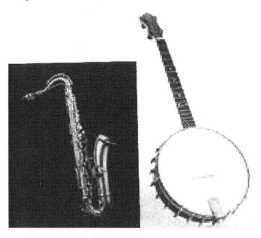

James Palao, Leader of the Original Creole Band brought the first sounds of Jazz from New Orleans to the south side of Chicago in 1915. The next ten years Chicago was the nation's Jazz capital. The banjo and tenor sax that he owned were donated by his daughters Clotilde, Agatha, Mable and Anita in loving memory of their father Jimmy Palao. Donated 7/10/1990 The saxophone was made by C.G. Conn, Ltd., Elkhart, Indiana Clark Street at North Avenue Chicago, Illinois 60614, Mrs Brownell /Olivia Mahoney Associate Curator Catalog Number: CHS, Banjo, 1990.382] Saxophone 1990.387.3a

Jimmy went directly to his family when he arrived in Los Angeles and he and Armontine began the rebuilding of their marriage. She said when she saw him he looked rather tired. She cooked him one of her fabulous meals. She was known for her cooking and she would set her table as though she were preparing for a King. This is how she acquired the nickname "Cookie". People would come from far and near to eat her Gumbo.

It is musically undeniable that the majority of musicians of the day considered Jimmy Palao to be one of the best violinists. Ed Dawson in an interview from the William Russell Collection stated that in his opinion, the best violinist was Jimmy Palao: Manuel Manetta was second: Peter Bocage was third: Francesco Valteau was next.(18) Mark Miller refers to Bill Johnson in a somewhat humorous sense, as "Cigar chewing Johnson". Johnson was already known to play the string bass in a vigorous pizzicato style signaling the music's transition from a 2/4 strut of ragtime to the forward 4/4swing of Jazz

Jimmy Palao was musically associated with some of the best trained African American musicians such as Manuel Perez and George Baquet. Testimony to the relationship with Baquet is a 1911 composition dedicated "To my friend George F. Baquet" titled "O You Sweet Rag" and "Echoes Of India". These are some of the very few copyrighted compositions from New Orleans musicians of this era. All of the musicians in the Creole Orchestra seemed to have lived a life of high social status and they were given professional music instructions (except for Keppard who couldn't read music).

Throughout the future years, Armontine remained suspicious of Jimmy and his involvement with other woman, regardless she stayed with him. Rebuilding a marriage after infidelity can be a very difficult and slow process. We do know he never regained the complete trust of his wife again. Jimmy Palao loved his wife and children. If there were any other indiscretions, Armontine was never able to find any evidence to support her suspicions. Armontine said she always sought her answers from the Church and clung to her faith to keep her marriage intact. She prayed constantly for her marriage to be happier, stronger and healthier than it ever was before. Armontine believed that God had heard her plead. She said "God has finally made me happy in my marriage." Jimmy nicknamed her "Papo" short for papoose. He believed that her love for him was like the love of an innocent baby, she was his papoose. She carried him, his words, his thoughts and his music in her heart all the remaining days of her life.

Jimmy made mention that Bill Johnson once said to him "If I had one woman like your wife, I'd give her all the loving that a woman needs." Bill was a good friend, yet, Jimmy wondered if this was advice or wishful thinking. He took it as advice. Armontine does make mention in an interview in a very gigglely fashion of one day after arriving in California, Bill Johnson took her around introducing her to everyone as Mrs. James Palao the moment seemed innocent enough. However it was noted as unusual for Bill to give that much recognition to any woman but his mother and sister and he never took his eyes off of her. (19) Bill does seem to be taken with Armontine who was oblivious to anyone but her husband and just so proud to be introduced as the wife of Jimmy Palao.

There was an account that traces the life of Jimmie Palao that was written in French, and later translated in English, the renowned jazz scholar, Robert Goffin stated: "When Jimmy Palao arrived in Los Angeles, it was he who sent telegrams to Baquet, Vincent, Keppard and Norwood Williams to come on to Los Angeles" Bill had set up more dance gigs for the Original Creole Orchestra to play in Los Angeles and Oakland."(20) Johnson knew he could call on Jimmy and the Band members would come without hesitation. These guys loved each other and they loved the music they played together. What a way to go through life enjoying every moment of your work.

According to historical records Bill Johnson had the features and even the voice of a white man and an unlimited sense of humor. Bill wrote to an associate "I have a white and very prominent father. My mother also is very light skinned – I turned out a white man, the rest of my family is dark. Anita my sister was light skinned to a degree though not as light as me." Perhaps his skin color helped him to get in places and set contracts, whatever the reason Bill Johnson was one of the best managers a band could have. . Bill provided an agenda, a schedule and a contract for every gig. He solely promoted this group, he believed in the new concept of Jazz. He had the professional skills and personal contacts, mutual respect in the music world. With his persuasive personality he was able to get the contacts and the money to finance the Original Creole Orchestra. He knew all facets of the music industry.(21) Although Bill didn't originally know all of the band members personally, Jimmy Palao did, and their reputations as being skilled musicians had followed them. Bill within the past three years had come to know them well Palao and Bill Johnson had a good rapport. It was definitely their time; they were a perfect match, the perfect duo. The Original Creole Band never roamed from club to club and he got top dollar. Bill Johnson could get into places where most Black American couldn't. Some say doors opened for him because there were times he passed for a white man but no one really cared because they were doing what they loved the most… playing Jazz. The Original Creole Orchestra was in demand; they could make the crowd jump out of their seats. Bill Johnson was also considered the father of the "slap" style of string bass playing. Johnson claimed to have started "slapping" the strings of his bass (a more vigorous technique than the classical pizzicato), after he accidentally broke his bow on the road with his band in northern Louisiana in the early 1910s. Other New Orleans string bass players picked up this style, and spread it across the country with the spread of New Orleans Jazz.

Jimmy Palao and members of this group all had grown up spiritually and musically, together in New Orleans. As though preparing for this moment for all of their lives, they had finally come together as a unit and formulated the Original Creole Orchestra. They had perfected their style. It took every one of them to make this happen, the formula was complete, the time was right, and everything was in place. The leader and violinist of the Original Creole Jazz Orchestra was Jimmy Palao, the manager was William Manuel Johnson. The members of the band were Freddy Keppard, cornet, Eddie Vincent trombone, Norwood Williams, guitar, George Baquet, clarinet, Danny Lewis- bass, William Manuel Johnson, bass Dink Johnson, drums,; Louis "Big Eyed" Nelson Delile, clarinet; Jimmie Noone, clarinet, Henry Morgan Prince, singer and dancer, Leonard Scott, singer and dancer.

The members of the Creole band began arriving in 1913. Baquet didn't join the group until after May 7, 1914 when he received his telegram. It seems Palao had difficulty locating him. He had moved and no one had a current address for him. It took a few months to settle in and they played several gigs and received great reviews. Keppard went back to New Orleans for a cutting contest that almost lost him his position in the band.

In 1914 Joe Oliver, Keppard's rival won a musical "cutting contest" and claimed Keppard's crown. Cutting Contest were established to "cut" another player on the same instrument and to replace him at his job by outperforming him.(22) Palao and Johnson felt Keppard was still the best and they rushed an offer for Keppard to stay with the Original Creole Orchestra and join them in Los Angeles, California. To say the least, Joe Oliver was mad as hell with their decision, because he felt he earned his way into the Original Creole Orchestra. Johnson explained that each of their Jazzmen were in the Musician's Union and the Union didn't adhere to the cutting contest rules.

The Original Creole Orchestra got its big break after the Leach Cross-Joe Rivers prizefight on August 11, 1914. In attendance was Carl Walker, manager of the Pantage Theatrical Company. When they played, "Mandalay", Freddie Keppard stood up with an egg mute and an old derby hat on the bell of the instrument, as he played the cornet the crowd screamed and screamed and screamed! When they finished Mr. Cal Walker asked for their card. He was so taken with their performance he arranged for an audition with his boss Alex Pantage, the theatrical impresario and the tycoon owned more than 30 vaudeville theaters and controlled, through management contracts, perhaps 60 more in both the United States and Canada.

The audition for Alex Pantage was a tremendous success. They appeared in their tuxedo's and Jimmy Palao played his violin with the melody high above, and each soloist improvised with unlimited melodic possibilities and then Jimmy ended the melody with all the others joining in. Mr. Alexander Pantage was so impressed he jumped up on the stage and asked them to sign up with him and he didn't care what they did as long as they played that style of music called "Jazz". Alexander Pantage signed the Original Creole Orchestra on his circuit vaudeville tour as a separate act. Vaudeville was a theatrical genre. of variety entertainment in the United States and Canada from the early 1880s until the early 1930s. Each performance was made up of a series of separate, unrelated acts grouped together on a common bill.(23)

There were in the middle of a two week break when on September 9, 1914 Armontine and Jimmy were notified that his Uncle Edgar had passed. They returned to New Orleans for his funeral. It was a traditional Jazz funeral, the band met at the church. Afterwards the band marched and led the procession slowly through the neighborhood streets. They heard the melodic strains of old Protestant hymns echoing through neighborhoods of shotgun houses and corner bar-rooms. There were black wreaths hanging on many doors in memory of Edgar Palao. The musical selection played was "Just a Closer Walk With Thee." The Brass band marched directly behind the hearse to the cemetery and the second line fell in step.(24) New Orleanians have been dancing to the beat of these brass bands since the late nineteenth century. These cultural traditions are not found anywhere else in the United States. This was Jimmy's last big family gathering with the Palao and Spriggs family in New Orleans.

They returned to California and the Original Creole Orchestra opened to a full house. Paul Howard originally from Ohio, was one of the top musicians in Los Angeles. He recalls when he first heard the Creole Orchestra at the Pantage Theater in Los Angeles. He said "He had never heard anything like this before. At the time he was working and going to school. He cut classes and didn't go to work just to hear this band. During their two week engagement Howard didn't miss a performance.

It was surmised by one historian that Prince Morgan traveled with the Original Creole Orchestra from time to time and might have been influential in getting the gig with the Pantages in 1914. Armontine seems to only remember that these men played so well that they got the gig all on their own. It was said that Prince despised Keppard's drinking frenzies and they didn't see eye to eye on most subjects. One evening in one of their heated arguments Prince took an object and hit Keppard on his head. Not long after... Prince took ill and never returned on the same stage again. It was thought that Prince was responsible for many of the popular dances of the 1920.s. However, I couldn't support these findings by verifying dates or definite information.

This new music "called Jazz "epitomizes certain elements such as, call-and-response, improvisation, and repetition, all are the "characteristics that make this music distinctive. It frees the sprit. [17] After a couple of tryouts at major loop theaters the Original Creole Orchestra was booked over the small Michigan vaudeville theaters known as the Butterfield time. They carried the Jazz of New Orleans throughout California.

Jimmy Palao was very charismatic, in his own way he got the attention of the musicians and they followed his every directive and then just at the right moment he would lift his hand and suddenly with the downswing of his arm the soloist would take off playing the tune as it had never been played before and he would say "Keep it real! " Just keep it real!" This was improvisation at its best... given all the right components of being at the right place at the right time... The most magnificent band leader of this era was born, and cultivated through his upbringing and environment. Jimmy Palao was an individual cosmic explosion that seems to have detonated in a region of empty space. Armontine said he captivated everyone he spoke to. He could walk into a room and instantly be the center of attention. He was a classy dresser and very physically attractive. He was about 5'10 in height, silky straight hair, olive toned light complexion and deep set eyes.

Jimmy had a quiet manner and he had mastered the powerful skills of communication and persuasion. He spoke Creole, French and Spanish. He loved hip talk better known as Jazz slang. He understood Jazz slang was an exclusive means of communicating freely in music, which in itself was a means of identification and gave all the musicians a sense of belonging to the group. They formed a brotherhood, a family, when on the road they sometimes slept together ate together and lived together and yet each was accepted for who they individually were.(26) Armontine recalled that Jimmy had a slight musical strut in his walk. She said "He just never stopped thinking about music, if he got a tune in his head he would play it over and over until it was perfect." He loved to hear his friends play and he believed in them and he loved Jazz..(27) Bill insisted that each band member join the Musician's union." The Musicians' Union, Local 208, owned their own a three storey building in Chicago. In the afternoons many musicians used to go over to the Musician's Union Hall at 49th and State St., to get jobs or just to hang out and relax. George Smith was the president of the local.

Jimmy Palao loved classical music and he was always impressed with the formal setting. Under his leadership they always dressed in formal tuxedos and presented a sophisticated music, known as "Jazz" to the world. They played and performed solos with one another that sent the audiences roaring. It was during this time that Jimmy Palao gave definition to the music he played and called "Jazz". According toa note on a postcard written to John Underwood he said "Jazz is a collective improvising free style music with a syncopated beat, using various instrumental styles and techniques, always starting and ending with the same melody." One of the most elegant times in America was this so called "Jazz Age". He brought Jazz to a higher status and the attire he chose was the tuxedo which was the sartorial mark of a true gentleman. They wore wing collared shirts, butterfly bow ties, sharply tailored tuxedos, gilts and paten leather shoes. It was a time when there was a taste for extravagant clothes. These stylish and well dressed Creole Jazzmen personified and up-lifted the new music known as Jazz to a new cultural level.. Jimmy and his aristocratic circle of musicians played a pivotal role in the elevation of Jazz. Temptations were great for all of them. These Creole gentlemen were good looking men, women of all colors and hues and positions… were all over them between sets and after. Jimmy Palao's elegant manners and high flown Jazz speech was better spoken and understood by Jazz musicians who created this new and infectious language Words like, hip, hop, cat and daddy- have helped contribute to Jazz's "cool" mystique. The new language better known as "Slang" was often used by the Jazz musicians to describe or express a quick direction. or Slang's popularity and power in American should not come as a surprise. By design, slang is wittier and cleverer than Standard English. Jimmy had picked up this way of communicating with the band from his uncle Edgar Palao and other Jazz musicians.(28)

The Original Creole Band traveled earlier and more extensively than other groups. People heard music like they never heard before, music that evoked emotional responses. According to an account from one musician who auditioned and withdrew from the band, "The leader Jimmy Palao conducted the 4/4 beat of Jazz like a metronome and if a beat was missed or skipped during rehearsal they would start over and they would play the tunes over and over until it was perfected. I never saw any leader of a band skillfully work his men so hard. I knew I couldn't fit in." There were many accounts that described his method of directing the band: it was said that Jimmy accentuated a few interesting techniques developed by the musicians for the playing of their instruments. What set aside this band from others and drew the crowds was their style. These musicians knew how to make their instruments 'talk'; it seemed that they were attempting to imitate the sounds of the human voice. You might hear one of the musicians while playing… shout out "Talk to me Baby!" or another caught up in the moment would shout out "I hear you talking!" It was said that: These guys were the advent of Jazz. They played their instruments as no other Jazz band had ever played before.(29) They used and developed muting, the growl, the shake, bending (or lipping), glissando, and fluttering. Muting is changing the sound of an instrument by blocking the sound with objects of different shapes and materials. The growl occurs when a musician blows and hums into his instrument at the same time. The shake is an exaggeration of the simple vibrato using the hand or movements of the jaw almost letting the instrument sound as if it were laughing.. Bending, also known as lipping, controls the pitch by adjusting the stiffness of the ambiture. Glissando, gliss for short is a slide from one pitch to another. Fluttering occurs when the musician vibrates his tongue against the roof of his mouth (as when one rolls an r). In other words, they played the hell out of those instruments.(30) These new techniques separated Jazz music from its predecessors. Jimmy Palao gave the members of the Original Creole Orchestra the opportunity to be known individually and the freedom to improvise and to develop a truly unique style of music.(31)

The first stop with the Pantage tour was in Chicago. The audiences went ballistic, when they heard the Original Creole Orchestra!!!

Chapter Six

Gained National Prominence
1914: Broke Racial Barriers

...Warm bloodied individual's thrush into the cold, without proper clothing, traveling on the road, not eating well, not sleeping, drinking too much and living in unsanitary conditions. Jimmy Palao and the Original Creole Orchestra, enduring all the odds and driven by the senses and the God given-talent and desire to please others with their talent. Determine to share and give life to a new music for others to listen to and enjoy.

Alexander Pantage had convinced The Original Creole Orchestra to sign up for an initial trial for a 16 week tour. The history of the Jazz in Canada begins in Winnipeg on a Monday afternoon on September 21, 1914, around 2:30 pm; six Creole musicians took to the stage of the Pantage Theatre, at the downtown corner of Market Street. The musicians listed were; Jimmy Palao, Freddie Keppard, Bill Johnson, Edward Vincent, George Baquet, Norwood Williams and Dink Oliver. Johnson. According to records Dink Johnson did not participate in the Pantage tour to Canada (1) The Original Creole Orchestra and its fellow acts proceeded by train in an autumn snow storm to Edmonton, Calgary, and Alberta. The tour moved to Spokane and Seattle returned to Canada in November for stops in Tacoma, Portland, San Francisco, Oakland, Los Angeles and San Diego before winding up in Salt Lake City in Early January 1915. In each city they were billed with Frances

Claire the dainty darling of vaudeville; Guy Rawson narrated the musical sketch "Yesterdays". The bill included the Great Harrahs a roller skating trio, the Irish Chatterbox, Arthur Whitlaw a monologist and McConnell & Niemeyer a song and dance team.

According to G. Ten Wright of the Canadian Edmonton Bulletin, "The big hit of the day was secured by the Creole Orchestra. Here a half a dozen culle'd gentlemen play slide trombone, cornet, clarinet, violin and bass viol...."Wright proclaimed the acts success later in the week "What might be styled the real hit of the show comes in from the New Orleans Creole Orchestra... After only six weeks on the circuit, it would be described by the Vancouver Sun as "the famous New Orleans troupe...." The significance of the band five weeks in Canada in1914 is symbolic; they were the first go beyond the major urban cities. They made their debut in New York in December 1916 and from January–May 1915 they toured with Town Topics. They later returned to Canada on this tour they took second billing to Jesse Lasky's society Buds a troupe of young women performing a musical comedy. The show also featured acrobats Welsh, Mealy and Montrose, a French Canadian slack-wire artist Kirtelli and impressionist Claudia Coleman

Jimmy Palao and the Original Creole Orchestra returned to Chicago for a two month engagement at the North American restaurant at Madison and State in the Loop. Then they performed at the Michigan vaudeville theaters, known as "Butterfield time". They were then booked by the Western Vaudeville Managers Association which grouped together several chains of theaters in Chicago, St. Louis and many cities in Illinois, Iowa and Indiana.(2)

Original Creole Orchestra; 1909 W. M Johnson, Manager Bass; Freddie Keppard, Cornet; George Baquet, clarinet; Jimmy Palao, Leader and violin; W. M. Williams, guitar; Eddie Vincent, trombone; Dink Johnson, drummer.

The Original Creole Orchestra brought the pioneering New Orleans style of Jazz to Chicago. They played the best of collective improvisation, each soloist improvised upon the harmony. Jimmy Palao as band leader "arranged" their music. These Jazzmen during their off time could be seen doubling or sitting in with other bands throughout the city. This also helped the evolution of Jazz, as they further developed the style and sounds of Jazz with other musicians. For many people, the lighthearted, improvisational sounds of Jazz were like nothing they had ever heard. Also, the music set the mood for partying and dancing, which gave many people a reason to be happy.(3)

African Americans had more power, women voted and people had extra time to perform and listen to the new musical sounds. It was Jimmy Palao along with other Jazzmen who first heard Lil Hardin play piano and accepted her into the band. She became the first woman to enter the Jazz field and became almost an instant major figure in the Jazz world. She retained that stature throughout her career. It was quite an accomplishment for a young college woman to be playing with the Jazz greats of her day and earning such a good salary.(4)

Chicago was becoming the focal point of the Jazz world. The most important clubs where the Original Creole Orchestra played Jazz were on the south side of Chicago known as the "Black Belt" located around 35th State St. Many of the clubs and cabarets were Black and Tan establishments where Blacks and whites drank, danced and socialized together, (this was considered a social taboo in other parts of town and most of America except for New Orleans). Blacks and whites walked "the Stroll", the name given to State Street between 26th and 39th streets. From 1910 to the late 1920s, thanks to the publicity efforts of the Chicago Defender Newspaper, the "Stroll" became the best-known streets in America. In one of their article in 1914, John Langston described the activities of these streets on the south side of Chicago; "The 'Stroll' was where the action was. This section of State Street was jammed with people night and day. In the evening the lights blazed and the sidewalks were crowded with patrons attending the clubs and those who stood just gazing at all the activity. During daylight hours it was a place to shop, loiter, to gossip and watch the street life. Black Chicagoans were on show and they dressed up in their best and acted accordingly. There was constant movement and noise which was once called Chicago's own city music; there was an endless stream of chattering pedestrians, street cars, horse-drawn carts and carriages rattling wagons of every kind and size and clanging trolley cars. The Chicago 'L' trains perpetually growled like rolling thunder in the sky, the musical sounds of the city never ceased."

Chicago was more of a cosmopolitan city than New Orleans and Jazz musicians found themselves playing for larger audiences than anywhere else. The Sunset Club was one of the largest Black and Tan clubs and was known as "Chicago's Brightest Pleasure Spot". Across the street was the Plantation Club and upstairs above was the Apex Club, A few blocks away was Lincoln Gardens with a dance hall for about 1,000 dancers. At 3520 State Street was the Dreamland Café it was a Black and Tan establishment. By the mid twenties there were literally hundreds of dance halls, theaters, speakeasies and a large number of cabarets (eating and drinking establishments) emerged on the "South Side". The opening of the hugely successful Savoy Ballroom at 47th in 1927 created a new center of Black nightlife. Chicago held a bigger attraction for musicians because it had more nightclubs than New York. (5)

Black musicians in Chicago formed their own Local 208. The two locals remained segregated until 1966. Local 208 was one of the most powerful Black musicians' union locals in the country, ensuring that a large membership of famous and not-so-famous musicians in Chicago would have access to jobs at standard wage scales. As more employment opportunities opened up in the North, especially in Chicago and the Midwest, musicians from New Orleans moved to Chicago. Prohibition and the advent of the "speakeasy" created many opportunities for musicians in small cabarets, dance halls and ballrooms.(6)

The Original Jazz Creole Orchestra led by James Palao continued their travels throughout Illinois and they remained in demand in Chicago. They went to the East Coast the later part of 1914 or early 1915 and invaded New York City. They played at the Palace Theatre and broke all box records. This was the first Jazz group to invade New York and they later joined Town Topics and positively stole the show. The "Town Topics" was followed by another trip around the Pantage's circuit, followed by twelve more weeks in the Midwestern theaters booked by the Western Vaudeville Managers Association.(7) They were hot! "Jimmy" Palao's, Original Creole Orchestra was the first musical organization to gain national recognition as they continued their travels. Bill Johnson told Armontine, "Palao worked the hell out of us and we enjoyed every minute of it". In putting the information together from several sources it was discovered that the Original Creole Orchestra would learn about ten or twelve new numbers a year. They had a repertoire of about thirty or forty numbers. Jimmy was constantly teaching and improving each band member's skills. The hot playing, improvising, came after they learned the number, usually as a 'head' arrangement. One man could go from one band to another and fit right in, with no trouble. They used to play the verse as well as the chorus on popular songs and most of the numbers had different strains to them. (8) We are still unearthing the truth from records of those whose living evidence survives.

Paul Howard moved from Ohio to Los Angeles in 1910 and became one of the city's major musicians. Fortunately, Paul Howard, the only musician whose memories remained of the group before they began to tour around 1914. Paul gave a very detailed description in interview of how the music was performed. "They, the Original Creole Orchestra practiced and practiced at the Clark Hotel every day." Howard was also impressed that the band did not play loud. A point contradicted by other testimony, notably from Bill Johnson, that in theater engagements Keppard was so loud the audience in the first rows was prompted to move further back. A bit further on in the same interview, Paul Howard recalled rehearsals in the home of Lee Larkins at Washington & Central Avenue which at times would get rather loud. Larkins was a friend to many of the Jazz musicians, and always provided a waist high keg of beer at the rehearsals. On an earlier occasion, Howard told William Russell that the band played a dance at the Central Labor Council Hall on Maple, between Fifth and Sixth Streets, in Los Angeles, and he heard their first piece, "The Egyptian." It was the first time he ever liked the clarinet in the low register? When Russell asked Howard what was their way of playing was called, Howard replied, "Swinging syncopation. They don't syncopate music nowadays" (Paul Howard). George Baquet said that the band members sometimes played between intermissions. Freddie Keppard, the master of the cornet, climbed up on a bench, put his derby over the cornet, and the crowd began to sway as he opened with 'In Mandalay'. "Get up in the ring and play, get up in the ring," an appreciative audience howled, and the Creole Orchestra would start before intermission ended. The incident was written up in the Los Angeles Times, where a cartoon of Baquet playing his clarinet was published.(9)

In January 1915, Armontine and Jimmy gave birth to Agatha in Los Angeles, California. The Palao family moved from California to New York around 1916 and lived there for about two years. This suggests that Jimmy had some notion that after the "Town Topics Tour" this would be a good place to stay. The Original Creole Band had the audience jumping out of their seats, as Jazz took hold, setting up a chain reaction, as they appeared in 75 cities over the U.S... Some of the cities were; Chicago, New York, Wisconsin, Iowa, Cleveland, St Louis, Washington, Oregon, Canada, Spokane, Los Angeles, San Francisco, Oakland and San Diego [See: Appendix Original Creole Band itinerary].(10) Touring activity of this sort during this era represented actual pioneering efforts.

Jimmy Palao always demonstrated his love for the music they created. He always allowed each band member to showcase his musical skills. A good leader knows that it's his responsibility to make sure that he gives the credit to the deserving person who did the great work. Jimmy recognized exceptional talent and did all he could to develop those individuals and allow them to be heard. He always got each of the band members to perform their best and this skill was a major contribution to the success of the band.

According to Guitarist, John Underwood, "The two things Jimmy Palao cared the most about were, his family and his music. As a Jazz musician he was a stickler for detail. He would hang on to every note. This was a guy who could work with people like nobody I've ever seen in my life, just within weeks of leading the band; he was able to draw the music out of their very souls. He had a good working relationship with everyone and all wanted the same thing. In the back of every members mind was the thought that people liked their music. Jimmy never met a stranger; he said every person he came in contact with was a potential friend or band member. He didn't appear to be scared or frightened at trying anything new with the instruments".(11) At first, it was tough because Jimmy Palao's expectations were so high. Every year, the band was getting closer and closer to rising to the top. It was basically a lot of work on and off stage, trying to make sure they were the best. In some ways, it was a lot of pain. Every day, they rehearsed in between playing gigs and Armontine remembered him saying it was really tough and he was beginning to feel exhausted.

Jimmy and Bill had worked together before and he knew that Bill knew all the clubs, bars, dives and venues. Bill had contacts that were eager to work with him in each state. He always made direct contact with the owners many of whom he knew personally. He negotiated the contract and money to be paid. The performers traveled together by train. Even though some rides were longer than others, they had a great time laughing and sharing stories. One conductor remembered in his memoirs, that the band members would sometimes harmonize a tune or two, they had great singing voices. Before the arrival of the Original Creole Orchestra to any event or gig Bill was given access to the stage equipment. He would hire a couple of the neighborhood youth and the stage was always prepared for their performance. The band spent their first season traveling with an act titled "Yesterdays" with six chorus girls a couple who danced on ice skates and a song and dance act by McConnell and Niemeyer

While on the vaudeville stage the band was reviewed at many of theaters where they appeared. Reviews in 1914 seemed at times to be muddled and were sometimes confused on how to express or approach this new art form without offending its readers. In the past only buffoonery in the entertainment field had been expressed in the media concerning Black Americans, now they were expected to go from the comic vaudevillian act to serious Jazz. Reviewers, who were mostly white didn't know how to review this Creole Orchestra and their music. The Breeze News reported, "Class may come and class may go but hokum goes on forever." In the same issue a Johnny Dooley is quoted as saying "...if slapstick humor and hokum comedy are presented in a clean, classy manner, minus any comedy makeup (Blackface), or any tinge of vulgarity... it seems the people absolutely prefer this to the exclusion of almost every style of entertainment found in the usual vaudeville acts." (The band had presented serious foot tapping Jazz).

The reviewers were having difficulty defining the difference between an expressive talented performance and the usual minstrel comedy show. The audience's reaction even puzzled the reviewers. On October 3, 1914 in Quincy Illinois they had booked a vaudeville act and the Original Creole Orchestra followed at the end of the act. The Quincy Review simply read: "The Creole band closed the show and closed it with a bang. Where do all of these colored gents get their sense of syncopation? It must be born in the bone. Such music was never heard; it was inspiring. The Creole Band is an act worth sitting through..." This was the first time a white reviewer gave proper credit to the Creole band and it was followed by many great reviews.(13)

I do not wish to in any way demean those Black Americans who sacrificed and presented their talent in the only form accepted from the years before. They paved the way; I have a special respect for the Black Americans who opened the doors for the oncoming multitude of future Black American geniuses. They provided the conduit through which Black Americans music, first reached the American mainstream. The Creole Orchestra on a couple of occasions shared the spotlight with a singer and dancer named Henry Morgan Prince. Prince taking the role of an old man cane in one hand and a jug of corn liquor and he sang favorites of the south Old Black Joe and my Old Kentucky Home. In the next scene he presented himself as well dressed and he sang and danced and got the audience up on their feet to learn the steps he took as they band played on and on. The reviewer said "the Creole Band played some weird instruments in a wonderful way." Henry. Prince Morgan seemed to only been on stage with the band, on and off for a little more than a year.

In 1916 George Baquet left the Original Creole Orchestra. It was said by one scholar who wishes to remain anonymous that the day he left the band. He locked himself up in a room and that only Eddie Vincent was allowed to enter.(14) The Original Creole Orchestra returned to Canadian theatres on the Pantage circuit with Big Eye Louis Nelson in Baquet's place, its performance in Victoria prompted this perceptive observation; "Nobody but six Negro eccentric players could shatter so many rules of music as we know it and make it so enticing to an audience, The cornet, clarinet, violin, guitar, trombone and double bass are played by individuals with seemingly absolute indifference to what the other man was doing but they always manage to arrive at appointed places in full accord." The Original Creole Orchestra was the first to take Jazz in its new form from New Orleans to national and indeed international audiences. I have taken only the reviews that clearly respected and understood and accepted this new art form as Jazz was meant to be understood.

I promised Armontine and Clotilde in my writings I would only present the factual and true information that would not in any way degrade or demean Jimmy Palao's journey and sacrifice to spread the music he so loved. Why would I or anyone chose to repeat and or interpret and analyze the negative bigoted comments and characterizations applied to a people of color and then attempt to express sorrow and then apologize. Those characterizations were based on ignorance and lack of understanding and total disrespect for these amazingly talented and professional Jazzmen. Let's "Keep It Real!" The only purpose reviews of this nature can serve is to give a date of a performance and the name of the group. I quote the following: "Racism does not exist in me or my thought or everyday living. It does not encompass me as a person. I have a personality a daily living pattern and a culture that dictates who I am.

Racism is out side of me it is not who I am. It is an unacceptable part of someone else's bitter thoughts that sometimes squeezes it way into my life. Racism is an annoyance, an irritation… a sickness.".

Managers loved good reviews: (my space is limited so I just sited from a few)

Seattle News was another matter, with a byline review that mentioned the band;

"The Original New Orleans Creole Band took the house by storm and won encore after encore. They are seven Negroes. Six of them are instrumentalist, playing the slide trombone, cornet, clarinet, violin and bass viol respectively. Their quaint symphonic orchestra struck the Pantages taste with a bang and so did their singing and dancing.(15)

A remarkable story surfaced from Oregon Daily Journal, 1916

"Four solid hours of entertainment given in the room of the Portland Press Club… The occasion was the Thanksgiving Jinks for the newspapermen and their friends and it brought out a large number of prominent men, including both and city and county officials… One of the biggest surprises of the evening was the appearance of the New Orleans Original Creole Orchestra from the Pantages theatre. After hearing the Band once, the audience would not let it go until the members had played every number they knew…"(16)

The trip from Portland to San Francisco was made by ocean vessel, apparently taking almost a week… The reviews were good. The Examiners 1916: *"The New Orleans Ragtime Band is one of the best things ever seen on the Pantages stage.' The Variety for the first time took notice of them "Pantages… New Orleans Rag time Band, entertaining…"*(17)

I must give credit to the Black newspapers who gave very positive insightful reviews. The Chicago Conservator Founded by Ferdinand Barnett (the husband of Ida B. Wells, Chicago, The Whip Founded by Joseph Bibb. the Chicago Bee Founded by Anthony Overton, Chicago Defender Founded by Robert Abbott, and the Pittsburgh Courier. The one that stand out the most was written in 1906 by the Utah Board Ax and the article was reproduced in the Chicago Tribune *"… the Negro has a future in music there is no prejudice in music… there is no prejudice against the Negro in music. He need not fear that race prejudice will antagonize him. Music is the universal art and language and begins where speech ends.".* This statement was written because, quite often journalists from the African American news media were not allowed in the some of the white establishments, where they may have had people of color performing.

Jimmy Palao had a vision and a personal belief and a set of principles. He made his dream become a reality he got the band members to work together, to act as one and to work hard. He was passionate about his work. He never lost sight of the fact that he knew each of the band members well.

There were obstacles for many non reading musicians from the beginning. In New Orleans, to be considered a good reading musician was given high praise and in Los Angeles the rules were more ridged, but there are numerous instances where the musicians were competitive and would not even work in the same ensemble if all the members couldn't read. The responsibilities of the hired orchestra included playing music before and after the show as well as accompanying other acts, and playing with other traveling performers. For some theater owners, the ability to read the music provided for the band was more important than the group's popularity or overall musical ability. When the musicians were given written arrangements to accompany other acts, if any of the members could not read the music the bands were fired. Consequently opportunities to play Jazz were limited because lack of musical reading training made professional survival impossible for many. Many musicians were not able to follow in the footsteps of the professionally trained jazzmen form the Original Creole Orchestra. (18)

Jimmy Palao loved the music and he worked hard to make others look good. Freddie Keppard was his best kept secret. For Keppard, was the one in the group who could not read music (which might explain why little is heard of him playing with big bands after the Original Creole Orchestra disbanded in 1918).(19) To compensate, he practiced by memory and he was so damn good he could fake his way through rehearsals and performances. He could pick up from the most complex melodies and harmonies with one hearing. With his remarkable range, he could do everything with his instrument. The way he played music almost ninety years ago would sound modern today. Jimmy Palao played the melody straight all of the time, up very high. If Keppard got lost in a tune, there it was up over his head, loud and clear. Jimmy was an excellent reader so he played the melody straight and high on the violin and Keppard improvised from Jimmy's lead. Keppard had two styles, cool and hot and his performances were so impressive that the show was often delayed until the audience quieted down. Not only was he a show stopper, but he was silver toned virtuoso, the voice of his horn was driving, dark and husky. Jimmy understood Keppard even though Keppards drinking was causing him at times to be less dependable, there was never a doubt that he couldn't blow. Keppard never missed a beat, his wild and ragged style of playing always put the audience on their feet. He talked with Keppard about his missing rehearsals, but he let him slide every time. Jimmy knew it was sometimes necessary to allow for individual faults as long as the performances were not affected.(20) Leaders are often expected to be motivators and enthusiastic and Jimmy Palao was both.

While playing under the leadership of Jimmy Palao, Keppard gained the reputation of being a technically very proficient player and an adventurous improviser. He was as good as Buddy Bolden. Keppard could hit the highest and lowest notes almost as good as the Angel Gabriel and he had marvelous execution. There was no end to his ideas and he could play eight or ten melodies… ten or twelve different ways. The mystic and reputation of these extremely handsome men who played this new music that sent you reeling and who attracted females of every hue and race only added to the curiosity of wanting to know them better.

Lil Hardin said: Keppard was a tall man, broad of shoulders, deep of chest; he had a heavy distinguished voice. The best insight to the personality of Keppard came from Mark Miller, trombonist a few years later. He said "Keppard was a tall, beefy light-skinned guy, and he was very conceited. He just knew that he was the best cornet player that ever hit the sidewalks of Chicago. Freddie drank all night, and the more he drank the better he played. He was actually a real good-natured fellow, always laughing and joking on the bandstand between sets. I remember how he used to strut in and out of the place, like a peacock, and he always dressed better than the other fellows, there was no counting all the suits he had". It was stated in book after book that Keppard thrived on the excitement of the crowd. Here is an excerpts in relationship to his musical performance; "…The applause from the patrons would bolster his ego and he would play louder, making the place really jump to the surefooted maneuvering that he performed on his horn.(21) or because of his disposition it was believed he wasn't capable of ever taking a back seat. He would take bows long after the band left the stage and he sometimes would begin to play a solo and the audience would go crazy." Jimmie would come and get him and they would go off the stage smiling and the audience was still applauding. Keppard loved the audience's response to his music and he loved all the applause and reviews that gave him the credit for the Jazz he played".

Eddie Vincent played the slide trombone in the characteristic tailgate style. He was a skilled performer. From all account: Eddie was a very quiet man and he kept a low profile, he didn't drink or gamble. He was known to have several women surrounding him and it was said he finally narrowed his choices down to one. I found no data showing if he ever married. George Baquet was well trained by his father, Theogene Baquet, clarinetist and Leader of the Excelsior Band. George in his early teens also played in the Lyre Club Symphony Orchestra. He was a master at effects such as growls and riffs. He was in demand and the audience loved his performance.

Dink Johnson was the younger brother of William "Bill" Manuel Johnson. Dink was born in Biloxi, Mississippi and raised in New Orleans. He was a multi talented musician, who played a swinging, piano but he worked magic on the drums. He played loud and he played creatively and exercised new dynamics using some of his quick perhaps faster-than-lighting-moving drumming skills, including off beats and syncopation, his hands moved at super speed... He demonstrated brilliant showmanship in every performance. Dink was known to have a rollicking, contagious sense of humor.

The only information I could find on W. M. Williams was that he was a guitarist; some historians seem to think he was under the name Norwood Williams. I found no information to support these findings, and there was only one description of W. M Williams that mention his profound renditions on the guitar. I also must mention that in the book Jazzmen is a poster with the 1911 picture of the Original Creole Orchestra that gives mention to a Bill Williams playing at the Chicago Grand Theater. So if Norwood Williams played the guitar for the Original Creole Orchestra let it be noted that in our findings he was an exceptional guitarist and his musical renditions are compared to that of Wes Montgomery (Musician of the next generation).(22)

William Manuel Johnson was known as a gregarious and resourceful manager as well as an exceptional bass player. Bill Johnson demonstrated inventiveness in his performances that would not be commonplace again until the rise of Charlie Mingus. Bill Johnson was very creative rhythmically and his playing is rich with alternating two-beat and four-beat feels, eight-note and triplet figures, and syncopations. He was rather known to be a ladies' man and according to records he had many wives. He was tall and he had amazing stage presence and he invented the technique of rhythmically slapping the bass while still strumming the notes and never missing a beat. These were the men who created the new styles of Jazz that would last for the next hundred and more years.

This was uninhibited Jazz at its best... Jazzmen demonstrating in their solos, that they have the ability to take the melody and spontaneously compose, edit, revise and reach the highest peak of performance. Jimmy Palao realized that these skills were the most important element by which Jazz players were judged. The crowds went wild during and after solos. This is what makes Jazz, Jazz. Jazz is the music that uses improvisation and it uses it to a far greater extent than any other style of music. Jazz required a good leader that will lead by example and be willing to do the work. Jimmy Palao was the man! This genius had developed a style of music that reflected the passion and creativity of an era. His artistry and energy changed the music landscape forever. America and the world have been profoundly affected by his originality.(23)

Armontine ["Cookie"] always spoke of her husband Jimmy Palao and anyone that knew her, got to know him. She brought life to the man in the picture and to his instrument that lay silently on the table. He became a real living person in a way that no clipping or photograph could ever reveal. It was at this point in my writings that I began to get a real feeling for who Jimmy Palao really was, not only a natural born leader. He was a energizer and he possessed, determination, self-discipline, willpower, and nerve. I began to feel the strength of his convictions the zeal he had for the musical talent he witnessed and the unconditional love he had for these musical giants and the music they created. He loved to discover and explore new musical ideas. He was a multitalented innovator. He quietly took every form of music in and gently cultivated and sculptured a new composition night after night from each of the band member's improvisations. Armontine said "Jimmy Palao loved how the guys worked with their instruments. Music was always on his mind. He talked and walked the music. You felt the vibe in everything he did, in every step he took."

Out of all the greats Jimmy Palao, seemingly, was the only one from many, of the musicians who encompassed the traits necessary, to have led the band across the country. He gave of himself, he went to homes and to the country down in New Orleans to help set up bands and he instructed many of these musical giants in their youth. He taught them how to play their instruments. He made these Jazzmen feel confident and relaxed. He could handle stressful moments and he seldom lost his calm cool manner. He was a motivator, an inspiration, he seem to take personal joy in letting others stage their talent. He was always focused on what worked best for the band and he was in tune to what excited and turned the audience on, and what they wanted to hear. He had a talent for simplicity saying things with a few catchy words and phrases to get your attention. [Better known as Jazz slang] (24)

A typical inclusion was Jimmy Palao's violin. According to Lil Hardin Palao was more than the fiddler of a polite Creole string trio. He too "could go back into the alley".(25) Jimmy Palao felt the need to express his Jazz voice through his main instrument, the violin. He was an accomplished and expressive Jazz violinist, earning a reputation as one of the finest Jazz violinists of his generation. He was able to execute powerful sounds that eschewed vibrato, phrasings and nobody had heard anything quite like it before. Jimmy's training involved violin lessons in classical music from a German woman, and Uncle Edgar Palao and his father, Felix Palao. Jimmy Palao loved listening and playing with other musicians and getting it all to work together. Jimmy Palao was multi talented, he not only played the violin... he played the saxophone, the alto, the mellophone.(26) *[WR Collection]* and the banjo, and he mastered them all. Charles Love in an interview from the William Russell Collection spoke highly of Jimmy Palao, the first band members he remembers leaving and going north was Eddie Vincent and Jimmy Palao. He said "Jimmy Palao was playing violin at the time and he also had played the mellophone in the Pacific Brass Band. He was a first class violinist and mellophone player. They tell me after he left here he learned to play the saxophone".(27)

The Palao Family moved from California to New York around 1916 and lived there for almost two years. Jimmy Palao was becoming a traveling musician who often seemed to live in trains, planes, taxis, hotel rooms, clubs, and in studios. He, like most of his colleagues, spent long periods moving from one gig to another. What it was like to be on the road all of the time?

There were many times they couldn't get a place to sleep. So they'd cross the tracks into the black section of town, pull over to the side of the road and spend the night there. They couldn't get into hotels. Their money wasn't even good enough. They would play nightclubs and spots which didn't have a bathroom for Negroes. They were often hungry because they couldn't buy food along the way and there were a number of restaurants they would pass where they couldn't be served.(28)

Bill Johnson never booked any gigs in Mississippi, Arkansas, or Alabama, Georgia, North and South Carolina. These were the states that had passed laws that interracial marriages were illegal and African Americans were being, beaten, thrown in jail, lynched and brutally killed especially anyone born from mixed marriages. Segregation and brutal racism prevailed in these states.(29)

A surprising number of Jazz musicians traveled the Gulf Coast network of waterways, railroads, and highways in search of greater employment opportunities in music. Buddy Bolden, for example, played on the Yazoo and Mississippi Valley line's excursion trains, which ran between New Orleans and Baton Rouge. Such trains stopped at LaPlace, where it was said that Bolden would play a number or two from the baggage car as advertising for an afternoon picnic and dance from 11:00 a.m. to 4:30 p.m. The music field was so big in Chicago; Bill Johnson started booking the Original Creole Orchestra three or four jobs a night. They'd play two hours (30) one place get paid for a day and got tips and then go to another and play another two hours.

Chicago paid more than New Orleans and Jimmy and the band members were doing great. It wasn't long before the New Orleans guys were taking all the work from the Chicago musicians. Chicago was particularly inviting because it seems that the musicians union there did not require Louisianans to undergo any stringent probationary restrictions in order to obtain a membership. Chicago placed emphasis on accurate performances. There were few bands that survived the brutally frank audiences only those who had mastered the skills of these Creole Jazzmen. In 1917 Jimmie Palao still a member of the Original Creole Orchestra doubled in the Lawrence Duhe Band. It was not unusual for band members to play with other bands. Sometimes the entire band played with other bands or on the bandstands with other bands. It was all about keeping a steady cash flow. In 1917 the Original Creole Orchestra had no bookings mid May to mid October, [see Appendix Itinerary] so members of the band played with Lawrence Duhe Band.(31)

This was ad in variety December 28, 1917 Billed next day as Seven Kings of Jazz. The microfilm from the library was so bad it was difficult to see.

These were happy times for the Original Creole Band. They had obviously made it in show business. One should observe that in a profession not known to foster marital stability, after some difficulties and a slight separation Jimmy Palao and Armontine Palao kept their family together. He provided for his own family financially and he also maintained a loving presence with his family.(32) Pops Foster said,

"We used to have a club of musicians of the twenty-five Saloon before we'd go to work and after we'd get off. There was Freddie Keppard, Jimmy Palao, Eddie Vincent, myself and a couple of other guys. When we'd get off work, we'd buy six drinks all at once for each of us. We'd drink them and go leaping home. Only sometimes we'd have to help each other out of the place. Most of the time after everyone met at the Twenty-five club, we'd start home."(33) According to Armontine Palao, Jimmie always came home around 3 or 4 a.m. sometimes a few of the guys slept over from time to time. Armontine said she only saw Jimmy play once. She also said her husband never wanted her to go to the places where they played music. Palao had developed a good relationship with Johnson, Keppard, Vincent and Baquet. They would come to the house and they were very nice men, always polite gentlemen, she enjoyed listening to them play. Armontine would cook her special gumbo for them and afterwards they would sit around and talk with each other and sometimes they would doze off to sleep.

The Original Creole Orchestra played in a pure, swinging New Orleans style and was quite successful. The audience frequently contained some of the leading musicians and stars of the day, including Bill "Bojangles" Robinson, the vaudeville team of Walker and Williams, Eddie Cantor, Al Jolson, and Sophie Tucker. Sophie Tucker, who was known to be interested in promoting Black songwriters, such as "All your Fault", by Eubie Blake **and** "After you' Gone" by John Turner Layton and many more.(34)

Jazz transcended significant racial barriers. Most danced to the music others listened, it moved, it bounced, and it was sweet melodies. Something else was quietly and joyfully happening, white patrons were found in venues which focused on Jazz, a form of music which often crossed the color line, recognizing talent wherever it was found. This music called "Jazz" helped to somewhat eroded racial prejudice. Musicians formed bonds based on their musical talent. Strange as it seems it was this mixture of culture that begin to bring people together. Many Black musicians looked upon Jazz as a way of removing Jim Crow barriers. Mixed audiences in northern urban areas began to put away their differences. Black musicians were opening in the most famous of clubs. It was almost a joining force between the people and if you were just that good, it simply didn't matter if you were a black or white musician, you could play where you wanted to and you were always wanted somewhere.

Jazz broke the rules musical and social. It featured improvisation over traditional structure, performer over leader, and Black American talent over unfair prejudice views. In the 1910s and 1920s Jazz firmly ensconced nightlife, the Depression era showcased the unique power of Jazz music to bring people of all races and classes together. This transformative experience in America through Jazz music was indeed remarkable. Here all races met on common ground and rubbed elbows as equals and there was an air of comradeship. It seems that Jazz music gave the opportunity to experience a society where racial differences were much less important. In time color lines were erased and interracial Jazz bands formed. Therefore Jazz should be remembered not only for its Jazz music but also for its ability to bring diverse people together. The racial and social mixing seen in and around America was remarkable in an era of racial segregation and class tensions. According to Eileen Southern in an interview it was this band that by-passed the strife and carried the sounds of Jazz from New Orleans to the rest of the nation. (35)

Everything's Copacetic… and the people really dig those sounds!!!

Jimmy Palao with daughter Mable 1915

Chapter Seven

The Ups-Downs and the Prolific Years of Jazz 1918 - 1922

Puritanical thinkers emerged in the United States during the era of World War I and the residents of New Orleans weren't exempt from these views. "Storyville", represented the epitome of sin and the politicians under pressure from the citizenry began tearing down the District. In October 1917 the houses of "Storyville" were completely shut down by order of the U.S. Navy, and a great many jobs for entertainers and musicians no longer existed. The performers began to look elsewhere for work. In the years following 1917, all the elaborate bordellos were demolished. Apparently, word was filtering back to the city of the success the New Orleans musicians were enjoying up north. Many decided to follow that example and travel north.

This takes us to early 1917, when The Original Creole Orchestra opened six weeks later under contract to Marcus Loew to whom they had been loaned to by the Marcus Bros. In Chicago January 8, 1917, a very brief mention in the St Louis Star dated January 9, 1917 read: "The New Orleans Original Creole Band with popular rags and southern melodies scored."

Of greater interest was the report in the St. Louis Argus and African American Weekly. "The private dance hall of Mr. Sam Shepard's place, 3634 Pine Street, was beautifully decorated for the banquet which was given in his honor by Mr. Geo. P. Dore, Tecumseh Bradshaw,

Robert Anderson, Alonzo Thomas and Sam Shepard. Fifty guests were present and had the time of their lives with plenty of everything to eat and drink, The Original Creole Band played the sweetest music that was ever heard in St. Louis and the guest enjoyed themselves until 3a.m.when everyone left feeling very happy".(1)

This African American Review was not the first to refer to the Jazz they heard as being sweet sounds. The truth being told that all Jazz is not loud, there were indeed Jazz Ballads. Jimmy Palao proved that the Original Creole Orchestra could play pianissimo (soft, smooth and mellow sounds) and could swing just as well and as when they played fortissimo (loud swing). One rendition the band jazzed up was a combination pieces the tropical sweet soft sounds of "Lotus Land" (by Cyril Scott 1905).. These were the moments you could have heard a pin drop amongst the crowd. Yet the performance that what was going on the stand was the most swinging sweet sounds you'd ever heard. I would agree with previous Jazz scholars that this was one of the indications of the connection of the band to the American community. The continuous applauding and roaring of the audience evidenced a pride in the accomplishment of the band that spoke volumes.

It was stated in the book "Jazzmen" that the Victor Recording Company sends a representative who offered Keppard an opportunity to record with the Original Creole Orchestra and he refused for fear they would steal their stuff. It was further stated that the Victor representatives offered a $25 flat fee to make a record (a fairly standard rate for non-star performers at the time), far less than what they were earning on the circuit per day. It was said Keppard was very vocal concerning the matter. His retort to this offer was: "Twenty-Five dollars? I drink that much gin in a day!" This story has continued by a few subsequent writers ever since and, probably due to a lack of evidence, it has never been seriously disputed. But what is the truth? The writers of "Jazzmen" do not quote any source for Freddie Keppard's words. George Baquet relates a different story. According to Baquet, Keppard began to become annoyed when the Victor Company couldn't record Bill Johnson's bass with the primitive equipment of the era and they also wanted an audition without paying. Keppard couldn't understand working without pays so Victor reclined the offer.

However, after extensive research I discovered that there was no record of a representative from the Victor Recording Company in 1915 approaching Keppard. The individual, if there was one that approached Keppard might have been a "music shark" in disguise: better known as a dishonest music producer, whose main source of income is the naiveté of new bands. Music sharks weren't concerned with royalties or long-term profit that would benefit the client, and or any actual promotion of records; rather, they devote themselves to making a "fast buck" by bilking as many as they can, in exchange for a big cut of the royalties or they sell your music to other producers because in the signed contract your music belongs to them.

The story recorded in a few books is that Keppard refused and he was paranoid and felt someone would steal his music. Keppard was by no means paranoid, he just wasn't stupid.. All of the band members had the right to be and should have been suspicious of others wanting to steal their music. It had become common knowledge that some unscrupulous white musicians and/or recording companies were attempting to take credit for the creation of Jazz music and they were aware that deals were made with others who gained the illegal copyright to music that was written by trusting souls. It was clear that fame and fortune was something which eluded many African-American musicians and bands due to institutionalized racism in the music industry and society at large. It was not uncommon for a Black Jazz band to record a tune to no acclaim, have a record promoter pay little or no money for rights to the tune, and then for that tune to be issued under the name of a white band to acquire national promotion and great acclaim. (Can you imagine, even Scott Joplin died penniless and his music is still on the shelves.).(2)

I was going over reels from the William Russell Collection interview with Bill Johnson and the truth of the matter was finally revealed. I found the following overlooked statement; Bill Johnson had an interview with William Russell on 12/19/1938. In that interview Bill Johnson mentions; that a record offer was made to him by Victor. He says it came through William "Bill" H. Vodery who was a leading Negro arranger in Chicago. In the interview he states that Bill Vodery could be found c/o Handy Music Company... This is the first reference I have found to a representative from Victor making contact with Bill Johnson. Bill

Johnson lived 100 years and it seems there were only two interviews done with him. I and another musical scholar connected with Brian Rust concluded that Vodery might have learned of the opportunity for a Black touring orchestra to make a record for Victor and passed on the opportunity to Johnson. Will H. Vodery an overlooked figure was one of the most respected well-known and best connected Black composers and musician in early twentieth century America. He did work for many of the most important Black and white stage figures of this era,. in 1915. He did the entire Ziegfeld follies show (one of the most Lavish productions in theater for that era), where he remained for twenty years.

Perhaps that started the conversation between Keppard and all of the band members that stated, they were against recording. Johnson from all we have learned about him was not one to close doors to opportunity, so he probably left the door open to negotiate later. This makes better sense because Bill Johnson was the manager of the Original Creole Orchestra and would have been the only one to handle and finalize all business negotiations and transactions.(3)

Armontine always insisted that Jimmy and the Original Creole Orchestra did record at least three records under Bill Johnson's management. She said Bill and Jimmy were approached around 1917-1918 and they were never paid. Armontine said that she once heard the music on the radio but he was never able to find out the name or title given to the music. She claimed that several of Jimmy's musical compositions were stolen and that Bill, Freddie and George and he had recorded at a later date, she was very convincing.

The British discographer Brian Rust discovered in the Victor files that a test recording of "Tack 'Em Down" had been made on December 2, 1919 by a "Creole Jass Band". (The session was entered as by "B. Johnson's Creole Jazz Band" into the standard discographies). Keppard left before the band broke up in late 1918, and it is not known if he was still with them at the time of this test recording. Baquet had left the band in 1917. "Tack Em' Down" was never issued under this name and by these musicians and no test pressing has surfaced. This would have been the first Jazz record was performed by a Black band,. The fact that this record was never issued or found, supports the theory that anything produced by a Black Band would just disappear. This was the most convincing evidence to support (4) Armontine's insistence that Jimmy Palao recorded with the Original Creole Orchestra and perhaps later around 1922 with Keppard. Armontine's historical accounts have been accurate so far and Lawrence Gushee a highly recognized Jazz scholar, found her to be a reliable Jazz source and all of her information thus far was proven to be credible.

A gig with Buddy Petit was confirmed according to the Chicago Defender, Jelly Roll Morton played with the Original Creole Orchestra in San Diego on February 23, 1918. Jelly Roll had grown up with many of the musicians and his wife, Anita Gonzales who was Bill Johnson's sister. It was assumed Jelly Roll and Anita were married to each other because Jelly often referred to Bill and Dink Johnson as brother in laws. There is also mention of this event in several books.

Armontine and Clotilde were able to locate only two of Jimmy Palao's compositions one was published by H. Kirkus Dugdale and the other by Carl Fisher.(5) According to Armontine these pieces were never distributed as promised and consequently Jimmy never received any royalties. When I researched the Victor recording records they claimed that they always stood behind their reputation and that they were always known to work with the musicians unions and guaranteed fair wages. Although after extensive research I must conclude as verified by Bill Sidran; "that the major record companies rarely gave Black artist royalties for their work".(6)

The Original Creole Orchestra was literally beginning to come apart in Boston. According to Robert Goffin; the band left for Boston and looked for a hotel to stay in vain and had to stay at Mrs. Wood's Boarding House. After a week there they were hired to play in Portland, Maine. They set a time to meet at North station. The baggage was checked with Freddy Keppard holding the receipts. Everybody was on time except Keppard, who was leaving Mrs. Wood's boarding house and thought it advisable to stop in a bar for refreshments. As he usually did he had the gin bottle set up on the counter and drank too much. When he arrived at the North station, the train left and the others insulted him and a terrible argument ensued. What could they do? The band couldn't get to Portland on time. They didn't have a job. The furious men reclaimed their baggage and sent it to New York, to the boarding house run by Lottie Joplin. According to Bill Johnson the end of the story differs a little... He remembers becoming angry after Keppard missed the train and he took the scenery and broke up the band returning to Chicago.

The exactness of this story is questionable, what is certain is that on Thursday April 26, 1917 the train to Portland from Boston's north station was missed... One can easily understand that Bill Johnson and Jimmy Palao were disgusted enough to call it quits after nearly ten years of traveling and the last four years were non-stop and grueling. There were stories from Miller, Gushee and Goffin that all conclude different details of the incident. However, it certainly explains why Bill Johnson did no bookings for the beginning of 1917. One can safely conclude he was sick and tired of Keppard's nonsense.(7) It was even wondered if the remaining musicians from the Original Creole Orchestra attended Scott Joplin's funeral who died a week before their arrival at Lottie Joplins boarding house. It was said that only a few were in attendance on April 5, 1917. Scott's musician friends wanted to play "Mable Leaf Rag" but Lottie said no, which it was felt she later regretted.(8)

During this down time in 1917 many Jazzmen from the Original Creole Orchestra joined the Lawrence Duhe Band which was an ensemble band that booked various bands or personnel as a fill in. during their off seasons. Lil Hardin gives the following account she applied for a part time job at the Chicago music store in the summer of 1917. The band members gave an audition by playing "Liberty Stable Blues" and she had never heard a band play like that. She said" they made goose pimples break out all over me. I'm telling you they played loud and long and I got the biggest kick out of the fit I was having over their music. They were booked at the Chinese restaurant but they needed a pianist and no one that auditioned could keep up with them, so Lil was sent over. ... The Creole Jazzmen heard her play and they hired her immediately. Four weeks later they were booked at the Deluxe Café (Thirty-fifth and State) and they made the unheard salary of twenty-seven dollars and fifty cents weekly besides twenty dollars a night in tips. The members of the band were Sugar Johnny - (cornet), Lawrence Duhe - (clarinet), Roy Palmer - (trombone), Jimmy Palao - (violin) Eddie Garland - (bass) and - Tubby Jones - (drums). The Band was a sensation from the first night at the Deluxe Café. There were no available seats after 9p.m. and a line waiting outside kept the doorman yelling at the top of his lungs, that soon there would be seats… These men played real New Orleans Jazz and the people ate it up. Lil said this was the most fun she had in her life. Everybody in town was coming in to see them perform.(9)

Excluding Lil Hardin, all of the band members returned to finish their tour with the Original Creole Orchestra. After nearly six months of inactivity with the Original Creole Orchestra, the group came together again still under the leadership of Jimmy Palao, for a final six months of Midwestern engagements in the Butterfield and the Western Vaudeville Managers Association theaters. It wasn't the same, the passion was gone and they couldn't recapture the moment. These six months apart from one another had allowed these Jazz musicians to envision and explore new opportunities and to perhaps realize it was time to move on. By the fall of 1918 the Jazz craze was in full bloom. Very likely it occurred to Bill Johnson and his band mates that despite its problems, the Original Creole Orchestra could still cash in on the steadily growing popularity of Jazz music.(10)

According to Jazz scholars The Original Creole Jazz Orchestra was perhaps the greatest organization in Jazz history of this era, until they disbanded the end of 1918. The members of the band together drafted a letter to the theatrical reporter for the Chicago Defender, Tony Langston. The following letter was received from the Original Creole Orchestra sent from Madison Wisconsin, dated March 8, 1918 it read:

Dear Friend Tony:

Just a few lines from the Original Creole band: we are all well and hope this will find you the same. Tony we have been out for five years and have only laid off five weeks and we think that is going some. It has been hard for us, as there were six Creole Bands out last year trying to do what we have done. We refuse to work for Harry Weber for small money; he wanted us to play the Orpheum time and said we would not play New York, but we did. We will use this act for the rest of WVMA for the time this year; after that we will go over to the Orpheum. We are closing every bill that we work on. Leonard Scott our comedian knocks them off their seats and all is well.

Regards to all friends,
Your friends,
Original Creole Band

This letter is a source of pride.(11) It is short simple and to the point but and speaks volumes. It shows strength of character and they certainly present a united front. The Original Creole Orchestra Jazzmen had to be strong and tough and also a little savvy to have successfully remained in the entertainment business for such a long number of years. This letter also gives witness to the fact that the Original Creole Orchestra's beginnings were before 1910-1911 and it provides intelligent sound reasoning for why the band broke up. According to the bands demanding schedule they already knew they were successful and their pocketbooks told them so. The crowds, roars and standing ovations gave them reason to know how good they were. They refused lower wages, knowing they could go on their own and earn more money individually without the expense and physical hassle of travel. This band had a good rapport with most of the circuits including the WVMA... as a gesture of fairness; they indicated they would complete their work with them. They made it clear that they could still get offers and proved it by getting their own booking in New York. They also didn't feel that the new bands posed any competition because they weren't doing anything new. The offer of the engagement for low wages wasn't favorable to them. They saw no joy in going broke for fame and no fortune! This letter acknowledges that they had paved the way for others to follow. They were tired, after a grueling five years with one break, they couldn't continue at this pace. There may have been other reasons but it was extremely satisfying to know that they stated the main reasons for their breakup in their own words. This letter serves as evidence that that even in the end, they were still working together and speaking as one. They deserve another standing ovation for this...

Vaudeville folk were a clannish group, more down to earth and human it seemed, than their counterparts. This loyalty and love which they had for their fellowman somehow showed in their public work. They had come a long way together after all the Original Creole Orchestra was the first Black American dance band to make transcontinental tours, on the vaudeville circuit. This band carries the "Jazz of New Orleans to the rest of the nation. Blacks Americans had taken control of their of the business side of their music from its beginnings. Through the protective music union local 208 they established a voice for themselves through contracts and collective bargaining agreements negotiated both locally and nationally.

Armontine remembered the evening that Jimmy met in their living room with Bill Johnson. They talked quietly for a long while. It seems they concluded that Original Creole Orchestra had seen its best days. They realized that the band members had given their all and had gone as far as they could together. There was a time nothing stood in their way. She heard Johnson say that, "The money is still good, the moments memorable, if we end now we come out on top and most of the band members have built a reputation that will take them on to higher grounds." It was Bill and Jimmy's belief that the guys could make the same money if no more than just playing the cabarets in Chicago, without the constant hassle of traveling. Jimmy ended with "If you ever need me call me, it has been great working with you." and there was silence…(12)

In the words of musical historians;"This Band established the first touring traditions that future bands would emulate". "The Original Creole Orchestra was the first New Orleans Orchestra to travel extensively, pioneering a path that would be followed by others." Despite the objection of a few, the majority of the Jazzmen voted on Monday, May 30, 1918 to disband and end all activity of the Original Creole Orchestra. There was mention of them being booked for the 23 additional performances. It was obvious that they had gained a lot of respect from Harry Weber and the other Vaudeville circuits. We don't know how happy their decision to leave made the Vaudeville circuits. The union stood behind their decision, they were guaranteed fair wages and reasonable working conditions as they pursue both art and a living. They parted like gentlemen did in those days … with a handshake.

The world had witnessed Jazz royalty at its best, even though James Palao and the Original Creole Orchestra made no such claim he really was the first "King" of these "Kings of Jazz" and they each individually earned the title.(13) All events and people are set in place for special souls to enter this world at a certain place and time. They follow a direct path and no matter what the circumstance they can't be stopped until their mission is complete. They go against all the odds. Everything is suddenly set in motion, the correct people and the right moment and with a driving force they have an lasting impact that will bring a change in the world. We have witnessed this phenomenon time after time. The Original Creole Orchestra had completed its mission and they had successfully spread the new art form called "Jazz" throughout the US and Canada

This photo was snapped on a new york city rooftop around 1917. The little girl is Jimmy Palao's third daughter Agatha born in January 1915

The Palao family returned from New York to Los Angeles and relocated to Chicago 1918. Anita Palao his fourth daughter was born January 10, 1918 in Chicago. According to Armontine, Jimmy seems to have taken his paternal role with his four girls very seriously. They were the joy of his life and when he was on the road he wrote them individual postcards and he always return with arms loaded with gifts for them. Clotilde remembered when her father was home he would play a little ditty for them each night before they went to sleep. He provided wonderful moments for them. He had no fixed income but he made very good money and he provided for his family in very good fashion. In 1919, a week before the riot in Chicago Jimmy had arranged to take his family to Milwaukee for a summer vacation. It seems On July 27, 1919, a young man was killed on the beach in Chicago and had set off a riot. People were killed, buildings burned, phone lines were cut, stores were closed and the National Guard was called in to guard the neighborhoods. He and his family packed their suitcases and they were taken to the train by Eddie Vincent on the morning of July 28.1919. This was the last trains to leave Chicago before the service was brought to a halt. The train was packed.(14)

Jimmy Palao worked hard and un-relentlessly in order to give Jazz a place and position in American society. Clotilde remembered them going to Milwaukee. Milwaukee had its own Bronzeville, most Black Americans lived in a confined segregated area in Milwaukee. Employment opportunities for musicians were somewhat good but the pay scale was much lower than in Chicago. They were beginning to dip into their savings and the racial turbulence had calmed down in Chicago, so they decided to return. Just in time for school to start in August 1919. (15) Chicago was well known for Jazz and the musicians were paid well and the tips were better than most places.

One day in conversation with his daughter Clotilde, she recalled asking "Daddy do you want to go home to New Orleans? He said "New Orleans is not my home anymore. My home is with you… and your mother… and your sisters."From this Clotilde and I concluded, "…once you have moved through the beginning passage of your life you can't go back in the physical sense. The memories are permanently in your mind, you can drive up the street you used to live on and reminisce about old times with friends and family. Suddenly you realize that home isn't just a house or a place. Home is in the heart and mind where moments, memories and feelings are stored; as long as you live and breathe you can always go home. Having a friend or family member to share and keep your memories alive makes living life much sweeter." Jimmy realized in his words to his daughter that he no longer longed for New Orleans. His wife, Armontine and his four girls, Clotilde, Mable, Agatha and Anita had become his heart and home. His father, Felix and he stayed in close contact throughout the years. Jimmy Palao's spectacular journey through this era made him one of the key figureheads in the technical mastery of this new musical artistic expression called Jazz. His reputation followed him and he never lacked for work.(16)

1919 – Lawrence Duhe Band at Comiskey Park, (Year of the Black Sox scandal). Left to right; "Ram" Hall, Honore Dutrey, King Oliver, Lawrence Duhe, Lorenzo Tio Jr., Wellman Braud , Jimmy Palao saxophone

Historical accounts of Jimmy Palao's travels are recorded in various books. In 1919 he rejoined the Lawrence Duhe Band and had the honor of being in the first Jazz Band to Play at a World Series game. It was the Cincinnati Red Sox versus the Chicago White Sox series of 1919. Members of that band were Jimmy Palao on tenor saxophone, George Field on trombone, trumpeter Joe Oliver, and Willie Humphrey playing second clarinet, Emmett Scott on banjo, bass player Wellman Beaux (Bread, Brieux) and Minor Hall on drums. The Lawrence Duhe Band played in Chicago at Dreamland, the Deluxe Café and the Pekin Cabaret.(!7)

Migration of Jazz men to many states after Storyville closed in 1917

98

1919-1920, Dreamland Café Chicago 33th South State St. Jolly Jazzing Jeopards; Lawrence Duhe Band; drums-Tubby Hall, tuba, cornet-Freddie Keppard Trombone- Roy Palmer, saxophone-Jimmy Palao, violin , violin , piano- Lil Hardin, clarinet- Lawrence Duhe. Originally published in the Chicago Whip December 27, 1919 (Courtesy of University of Chicago, John Steiner Collection)

Lawrence Duhé and his New Orleans Creole Jazz Band and his pianist, (Lil Hardin); toured as an ensemble which featured various Jazz bands. Sugar Johnnie Smith died of pneumonia, late of 1918 and Mutt Carey, musician, came to replace him. Jimmy Palao was asked to rejoin the Band, early January 1919; this was the first time that Joe Oliver and Jimmy Palao played in the same band. The Lawrence Duhe Band played in the World Series October 5, 1919 in Cosmisky Park. Mutt Carey couldn't stand the cold, so he quit the band. Joe Oliver replaced him in December 1919. Keppard warned Jimmy about Oliver. Joe Oliver had acquired a reputation of having a bossy and authoritative streak. There was trouble in the band around late 1919 and Duhe left.

After a very heated verbal discussion with shouting among the band members Oliver assumed leadership. A few weeks later Joe Oliver renamed the Lawrence Duhe Band the 'King Joe Oliver Creole Band'. Bill Johnson who handled the business side of things even though he no longer had a band was still booking shows in California. Johnson knew that Jimmy Palao was playing with this band and he spoke with Jimmy. Joe Oliver **and** the "King Joe Oliver Creole Band" were then called to

California by Bill Johnson. It might be easy to assume that Jimmy Palao was responsible for the call from Bill Johnson, even though I could find no evidence to support this it is feasible.(18)

The work in California was lucrative and the King Joe Oliver Band .signed a contract with the Pergola Dancing Pavillion in San Francisco which called for the seven piece orchestra, consisting of Joe Oliver, Honore Dutrey, John Dobbs, Lil Hardin, Minor Hall, Edward Garland, and James Palao. The contract read: "The band shall play continuously, dance music as played in so-called "nickel dance" as directed by the party of the first part between 8 pm and 12 pm" The contract also covered a six-month period extending from June 21st to December 21st. (1920). This dance music had become popular all over the world. This music captured a moving fluent motion, full of steps, kicks, leg pumps. Dances included the Tango, Shimmy, Waltz, the Charleston, Cake-Walk, the Turkey Trot, the Black Bottom, and the Bunny Hug. With the increasing popularity of dances, Jazz became more and more popular; events such as dance marathons were also created. The 1920's, this period of time became known as the "Jazz Era, The Roaring Twenties".

It was recalled by Floyd and Buster Wilson that King Oliver Band came to California in 1921. They were invited to Wayside Park and Levin himself recalls that in an early interview with Reb Spikes, "He told me that the King Oliver Band with Wilson on piano made a few recordings in Santa Monica for the Spikes brothers on the Sunshine label"(20). He assumed that the master copies were among those that melted during shipment across the hot desert to an eastern pressing plant. Also Jelly "Roll" Morton's reunion with these most dominant musicians of all time must have had a powerful impact on Jelly's life. Not to mention that King Oliver's Creole Jazz Band included Jelly Roll's old friends and acquaintances from New Orleans, Johnny Dobbs, clarinet; Jimmy Palao, violin; Honore Dutrey, trombone, Lil Hardin, piano; Minor "Ram" Hall, drums; and Ed Garland, bass; (Garland stayed on the west coast and Bill Johnson filled in Chicago). Morton said he felt honored to be surrounded by musicians of that caliber. One wonders if this had an influence on Morton's decision to return to Chicago.

1921 King Oliver's Creole Jazz Band. Left to right; "Ram" Hall-Drums, Honore Dutrey-Trombone, King Oliver-Cornet, Lil Hardin-Armstrong-Vocalist, David Jones-Saxophone, Johnny Dodds-Clarinet, Jimmie Palao-Violin, Ed Garland-Bass Violin [7-95] King Oliver's Band playing on the sidewalk in San Francisco, California. Lil Hardin Named all of the band members in this picture and she knew them all well.

Perhaps a little background on Oliver will help to explain his disposition. Oliver was blinded in one eye as a child and often played while sitting in a chair, or leaning against the wall, with a derby hat tilted so that it hid his bad eye. Joe had to fight all of his life and perhaps even bully others to be heard. Joe was famous for his using mutes, derbies, bottles and cups to alter the sound of his cornet. He was able to get a wild array of sounds out of his horn with this arsenal of gizmos he played hard and well.(21)

There were continuous disputes between Oliver and Jimmy Palao. Oliver's instrumentation was boisterous and loud. Some people seemed to enjoy his rather comic style. Joe couldn't give up the farm clothes and the southern country slap stick humor. This went against Jimmy Palao's thinking. It was the one time that Armontine, came to see them play. She was disappointed they were such good musicians, she questioned why would they dress like that?(22) The King Joe Oliver Band as depicted in the picture above [7-94] wore country costumes as depicted in the minstrels, pen collared white shirt, red undershirts, suspenders and the disputes continued between Jimmy Palao and King Oliver.

Most of the band member's had remembered Oliver was becoming more and more difficult and unpredictable. He insisted on discipline in his groups and he made the band members aware that he carried a pistol in his briefcase with his music. Oliver didn't want any of his band members to out star him on the bandstand. He made sure that their solos were fewer and shorter than his. This concept totally and completely went against all that Jimmy Palao had accomplished in assimilating and transforming the musical formation of Jazz. Jimmy wanted every factor of rhythm; phrasing, improvisation, harmonic voicing to stand out and he knew no one person possessed that talent. As leader of the band he always got others to produce their best and he gave each man an opportunity to display his talent to improvise and to star with each solo. He knew that each man was an asset and a necessary success to the music called "Jazz". Improvisation and letting the musician's natural talent shine in their solos was an incredibly complex procedure that encompassed every element of Jazz and the music itself… but he was not leader of this band.

The augments continued and were becoming worst… Palao felt Oliver just wanted to showcase his own talent. He just didn't get it… he was set in the old ways and didn't understand or grasp the concept of Jazz. Each time Armontine and Clotilde told this story they would become angry with Oliver as though it happened yesterday. They said Jimmy had tolerated King Oliver's grandiose behavior for too long and he openly spoke out to Oliver. They alternately quoted him as saying "We are musicians' man; either the people accept the music we play as a statement that speaks for itself, without all that Uncle Tom shuck-and-jive, or forget it. I have worked hard to get people to take us seriously. You got us dressing like country bumpkins and yet you stand there in a suit and hat at all times. You are taking us a step backward. It's not about you, it's about "Jazz". Can't you see how the music has grown? Man wake up! We will come and go. We want "Jazz" to stay and everyone who played it to be remembered!" He said a quick, sudden kind of a tremble went across Oliver's face that Jimmy/Papa said he would never forget.(23)

This is the only time Oliver was quiet. A few days later after this outburst Oliver fired Jimmie Palao without notice and without return fare to Chicago. Minor "Ram" Hall quit because of this and Oliver had Baby Dobbs come in from St. Louis. Oliver didn't consult with the union about firing Palao and replacing the drummer (Minor "Ram" Hall). The union [Local] 6, [S.F..] forced Oliver to give Palao two weeks with notice and pay for his fare back to Chicago: Hall had to stay with the band that two weeks also and Oliver also had to pay his fare to Chicago. In addition Oliver was fined $200.00 for not obtaining permission from the union to import the violinist and drummer. We do know that this was the last time the King Oliver Band was seen dressed in country attire. From that day forth they were only dressed in Tuxedo's and dress attire. Bill Johnson who handled the business side of things as well as bass playing in the band was still booking shows. He found himself with a gig at the Royal Gardens (469 East 31st Street) in Chicago and no band.(24)

At this point he contacted first Buddy Petit, and then King Oliver. Oliver had added Louie Armstrong and he quickly reconstructed the band and the newly formed King Oliver Creole Jazz Band and went back to Chicago to open with a fifteen piece band at the Royal Gardens. Of course Oliver hadn't paid the fine of $200.00 he owed; consequently every member of that band was fined $100.00 each by the union: The operator of the Royal Gardens had to collect and pay the fines before the band could open in Chicago. When Oliver went to the big city of Chicago's even though the band was good, he apparently completely forgot his roots. I believe this was the last of the Creole Bands. It isn't clear if Johnson went with Oliver to Chicago. We do know that Bill Johnson established his own band at a later date. Bill Johnson began to play with the Wycliff Gingersnaps or the backup band for Dave and Tressie

After the King Oliver's Creole Band cut its 1923 sides, Oliver begin saying "my band" rather than "our band." He began to take more control and see himself as the only star. He began turning down gigs because the pay was too low. During the recording, those present - especially pianist Lil Hardin, recognized that Armstrong could outplay Oliver. In any case, Louis began to upstage Oliver, though he never intended for that to happen. Louis Armstrong was so talented and Lil Hardin feared for his safety with Joe Oliver. She just wanted to get him away from Joe, out on his own. Oliver's overly rigid procedures and his unwillingness to evolve along with the Jazz idiom caused most of his players to leave, seeking an atmosphere more conductive to new ideas.

Lil Hardin and Louis Armstrong announced their wedding plans. Jimmy Palao was present at the wedding reception February 7, 1924, in Chicago at a time when Dave and Tressie and Jimmie Palao was traveling there with the Gingersnaps.(25) Interestingly enough, Bill Johnson and Joe Oliver were not present at their wedding. In mid 1924, with the support of Lil and other band members, Louis left the King Oliver Creole Band and he played for a few months in 1921 with the John H. Wickliffe Gingersnaps as pictured. Jimmie Palao is in the same band. Armstrong played with numerous bands during this short period before signing with Fletcher Henderson in New York, where his stardom began to rise.

1921 John Wickliffe band; John Wickliffe on drums. Jimmy Palao violin third from left, Louis Armstrong playing saxophone to left of picture (This picture on a postal mailing postcard published for advertisement 1921.

On back of this mailing card, reads the following: Famous Ginger Band of Chicago, Ill./ Kings of Cyncopation and Harmony/ Every Man an artist / Milwaukee Journal ;(26) Wickliffe's Band, will make an Egyptian Mummy dance./ Chicago Tribune,(27) Wickliffe's Band, a great bunch of Southern Artists./ Tw… at the Morrison Hotel and Terrace. The Entertainer's Café Chicago/ … of the Ballroom. [This card indicates that the artistry applies not only to musical ability but also their singing ability.]

Many of the Jazz musicians returned to New Orleans because they found the weather conditions in Chicago unbearable. The Hawk will get you, derivation of "Hawkins," meaning a bitter wind, something disagreeable, or a bogeyman. Everyone talked about how bad and terrible the winters in Chicago were. Temperatures seem to be always below freezing or in the tens and twenties. It was difficult to survive a Chicago winter by someone moving here from a warm southern state who had never dealt with extreme cold, wind, snow and ice. People and cars can't avoid being cold and stuck somewhere during a blizzard.

It was unbearable getting un-stuck from the snow and navigating through icy streets with a wind chill that makes it seem 20 degrees colder than it already is. Even with 3 feet of snow, school, work and the stores do not close down. The big snows come mostly in December to March and it happens every year. Chicagoan's dig out the cars and buses, take public transit, shovel the sidewalks and driveways and bundle up and go out slowly and cautiously either by car or by foot... Northerners' have no respect for bad weather they just keep going... nothing stops... in Chicago.(28)

Jimmy Palao had spent what seemed like a lifetime away from his Louisiana southern home, forcing him to new audiences with the music he had learned back in New Orleans, rethinking and reinventing himself, exploring his musical capacities and creating new meanings while on the move. He missed the warmth of Louisiana and its tropical terrain. He boarded the Illinois Central train to travel to return Chicago, to his family and perhaps where he decided to stay and weather the storm. (29)

The puritanical attitudes began to clash with the new found physical freedom of Jazz, combined with the illicit mix of races and the widespread belief that jazz stimulated sexual activity, caused critics of jazz to step up their efforts. "Jazz was thought to be originally the accompaniment of the voodoo dance, stimulating half-crazed barbarians to the vilest of deeds," proclaimed Ann Shaw Faulkner, president of the General Federation of Women's Clubs, a powerful alliance of women's social and reform groups who launched a crusade against Jazz in 1921. The reformers couldn't fight progress. Jazz recordings had reached beyond the nightclubs and the music flourished....

A picture was provided to me of the A. J. Piron's Orchestra indicating that the saxophone player was Jimmy Palao. I wasn't sure of this so I didn't publish the picture I went through countless interviews and books. Piron seems to have had a close connection with Jimmy Palao maybe they were rivals who respected one another, I am not sure. I happened upon the interview of Johnny St Cyr who only became acquainted with Jimmy Palao after 1918. In his interview he provided evidence that Jimmie Palao took over Piron's position in the Olympia Band. I found several pictures of A. J. Piron in his youth and later and I have yet to find any evidence that Jimmy Palao played in any of his bands. Although I happened upon a picture of A. J. Piron playing in the Excelsior Brass Band and Felix Palao is also pictured playing the saxophone. I have a picture Felix Palao playing the Excelsior Brass Band in this book. I found nothing to indicate that Jimmy and A. J. played in the same band at the same time.

One night at Lulu White's Economy Hall, Piron went down on the floor during intermission to talk to a girl he knew. Freddie Keppard hollered to him, 'Come on man, we've got to play some music.' Piron called back, 'Don't yell at me, man.' Piron got real hot about this and he put his violin on his chair and refused to play. During the course of the number, he forgot his violin was on the chair, and he sat on it. The members of the band laughed so hard, he packed up and went home. That was the last time he played with the Olympia Band — Jimmy Palao took his place. Keppard and Palao set in for a one night gig with the Olympia Band in 1912. They were in between bookings and doing a double shift. Afterwards Keppard and Palao returned to the Original Creole Orchestra to finish their arranged bookings.(31)

In 1922 record companies such as Columbia, Paramount, and Vocalian began to seek out popular African American bands to record their works. It was not until 1922 that record companies became convinced that African American musicians would be popular with the consumer market. Production of subsequent "Race records" proved to be extremely lucrative for record companies. These "Race Records" were 78 rpm gramophone records made by and created for African Americans and recorded by African American musicians. Major recording areas were New York City, Camden, New Jersey, and Chicago. They were marketed by Okeh Records, Emerson Records, Vocalion Records, Victor Talking Machine Company, and several other companies many of which were branches of major companies. During the time, "Race records" were produced, there are three recordings under Keppards name.(32)

Digitally re-engineered recordings remove all of the sound imperfections such as scratches and distortion and now allow us to hear and appreciate the sounds of those who recorded. I was surprised by the wonderful renditions that Keppard and the Jazz Cardinals played. I believe that we could be hearing some of the Original Creole Orchestra Jazzmen playing with him such as Bill Johnson slapping the bass and Jimmy Palao on violin. I conclude this because I originally could find no record of any group called the Jazz Cardinals.(33) The record companies sometimes would use other names because they didn't want give credit to a group of Black Americans. Also there were not that many musicians that could duplicate the sounds from these proficient Jazzmen. It must be noted that Keppard was a little clannish and was not always comfortable with others. It must also be remembered he didn't want others to know he could not read music. .Perhaps these were some of the recordings mentioned by Armontine Palao.(34). However a few days ago on an internet data base just as I suspected the names of the Jazz Cardinals were listed and I will need additional time to research and confirm this new found information If this information is accurate it will confirm the information given by Armontine Palao that Jimmy Palao recorded with Keppard.

The prolific years of the 1920's known as the Roaring Twenties was alternatively known as "The Jazz Age". This was the "movement" in which Jazz music grew in popularity by immense standards all over the world.

Jimmy Palao 1920

Chapter Eight

The Last Days of Jimmy Palao

Eventually Jimmy Palao returned to the Midwest, touring in the last years of his life he joined the "Syncopated Gingersnaps: the band with the singing and dance duo of Dave and Tressie. Jimmy was hitting the big time when he was booked by David and Tressie and Band headlined the WVMA (The Western Vaudeville Managers' Association) and B.F. Keith Circuits in the East [out of Chicago].(1) B.F. Keith Circuits controlled all of the theaters and fairgrounds in the Midwest and the Midwest and the Orpheum on the West Coast. The WMVA and the Orpheum soon merged. The WVMA was considered to be the "junior circuit" and only booked acts on the way up.

Dave (Stratton) and Tressie (Mitchell) had been a dance team from 1921 on, they announced their intention to add a Jazz team to their act early 1921 (Billboard, January 7, 1921). This may not have happened until 6 months later, when an ad in Variety referred to Wickliffe's Gingersnaps as their seven piece Jazz band. Fess Williams was a master of the stove pipe clarinet, [the uncle of Charles Mingus] also toured with the variety song and dance act of Dave and Tressie around 1922. Doc Cook and his 14 Doctors of Syncopated Gingersnaps were also known as Cook's Dreamland Orchestra was one of the city's leading African-American dance ensembles. Jimmy Palao was one of the Syncopated Ginger Snaps. A band so name to describe of the color of the musicians skin, and of the finger snapping syncopation of their music. A newspaper article dated later refers to "Dave and Tressie as eccentric dancers. Dave and Tressie were professional colored dancers on the opening at Columbia today. The music for the dance number was supplied by the 'Syncopated Gingersnaps". Traveling shows of this sort were generally pretty well received.

Sycopated Gingersnaps Jimmy Palao saxophone , first seated left to right 1921

Sycopated Gingersnaps Jimmy Palao standing left of June
Clark and Tressie and Dave at the top 1922>>

The joy of sharing and developing Jazz took its toll on "Jimmy's" health. The symptoms of that disease included a persistent harassing dry coughs which Lil Hardin mentions that Jimmy had. That cough eventually led to "hollow rattles" known as the "graveyard coughs." Jimmy endured the chest pain and shortness of breath, weight loss, spitting of blood, hoarseness, night sweats, increased pulse rate and fever for as long as he could. But now he couldn't stand for long periods of time. Tuberculosis was called a "house disease" and citizens were urged to practice hygiene to prevent it. Unfortunately, many Jazz musicians were stricken with Tuberculosis due to the unsanitary living and working conditions of being on the road only hastened the spread of the disease. Many of the musicians were unable to eat clean or properly prepared food and they often slept in crowded unsanitary dwellings. They worked long hard hours in the cold and damp environments in the winter and stifling hot conditions in the summer.

Jimmy Palao and Eddie Montudi Garland

Jimmy Palao was on the road with The Syncopated Band and Dave and Tressie, when it was realized Jimmy's condition had worsened. Although, Bill Johnson may have temporarily left the band and returned, it was he who informed Armontine of Jimmy's illness and the need for him to return home to Chicago. On November 29, 1928 his illness was so advanced by time he reached Chicago that he could barely get off the train. He didn't make that ride alone. Bill we were told went to New York and rode the train with Jimmie all the way to Chicago.

Postcard Dave and Tressie

Armontine didn't see them on the boardwalk she talked the conductor into letting her on the train. Jimmie was very thin almost swallowed up in his suit. Bill and Armontine helped Jimmy from the train. Bill, Jimmy and Armontine caught a cab home, to 5485 S. Woodlawn. By the time Jimmy climbed the apartment steps he could barely breathe. Bill left to board a train back to New York. Armontine remembered tears in Bills eyes as he hugged her and left. The children sat outside the room in chairs where they could see him and they talked to him and told him they missed him and they loved him. Each day Jimmy would sit in the chair in the bedroom and play his violin and banjo. Armontine would go to the store and she would hear the sweet music from his room when she was returning. It amazed me that this musician, who gave so much of himself and spent years working on his craft, figuring out ways to bring Jazz to the people: surrounded by the shouts of people would come to his end in such silence.(3)

Tuberculosis was responsible for many deaths during the early 1900's. Some patients died quickly or lingered as invalids for years; some recovered, but no one could determine, when or if the disease would strike again. It appeared that after Jimmy was home he was improving. He gained weight and he stopped coughing… One afternoon she heard him playing the saxophone. On December 21, 1928, Armontine returned from the store and there was silence. He lay on the bed unable to catch his breath. The disease had returned with a force. Jimmy was coughing blood. She called the doctor. The children arrived home from school and Clotilde and Agatha remembered seeing their dad lying on the side of the bed and his eyes appeared to be bugling out. Agatha kept crying "he's dead my daddy is dead!". Armontine assured the children he was okay and told them to keep praying.

Armontine took the children to a neighbor. The doctor came and insisted that Jimmy go to the hospital. Jimmy's hands were trembling, she said she held his hand; he looked at her, touched her face and hair and beckoned for her to come closer. He whispered "I love you" and the attendant placed him in the ambulance and took him away. The doctor was mandated to report the situation to the Board of Health; just in case Jimmy didn't survive she was assured that the Bureau of Vital Statistics would issue a death certificate since the case was reported.

She was told she couldn't ride in the ambulance and that it would be a few days before she could see him. They were going to quarantine him in the infirmary of the hospital. She was told to disinfect the areas he had touched and there would be someone out to inspect the premises. Jimmy had confined himself to the bedroom for his brief stay at home. She went through the room and threw all rags, cloths, paper, blankets, linen, pillow cases, curtains, hangings, draperies, rugs, shoes, gloves, personal clothing, in a big metal container and took it to the back yard and set it on fire until everything was burned to a crisp. She scrubbed the mattress and managed to get it out the back door and threw it over the banister and she went down the back stairwell and pulled the mattress into the alley and set it on fire…

She hadn't unpacked the trunk with the pictures, music and books he came home with .She scrubbed and stored his instruments away with his other belongings in the trunk, in a dry place, which in time without light all germs and bacteria would die. Nothing was left in the room but an iron bed. She had worked non-stop for 12 hours and she was exhausted. She then went to the bathroom ran the water and she scrubbed her body and hands as she cried and cried and cried.

The doctor had Jimmy immediately transferred to a hospital where he remained for two days and then he was transferred to a sanitarium where he stayed until January 6, 1925. He was then transferred to Cook County Hospital where he passed away on the morning of January 8th, 1925. He was little more than a month short of his forty-sixth birthday. His wife had remained dutiful and loving and stayed by his side until death.

Four days later he was buried in Mount Olivet Catholic Cemetery. Located at 2755 W. 111th St. Chicago, IL 60655, Mt. Olivet was the first Catholic cemetery on the South side of Chicago. His four daughters stood beside their Grandfather, Felix.. There wasn't a big crowd of mourners; there were many curious spectators who recognized many of the musicians. Just to name a few in attendance, Bill and Dink Johnson, Lil Hardin and Louis Armstrong, Anita Gonzales and Jelly Roll Morton, George Baquet (flew in from Philadelphia), Sidney Bechet, Ram "Minor" Hall and many other well known and local musicians were in attendance. The guitarist Johnny St. Cyr recalled that it was extremely cold on the day of Palao's funeral. He, Jimmie Noone and Freddie Keppard went there in an open car but mistakenly joined another cortege and wound up at a different cemetery two miles short of their goal. It was so cold they were among the few who decided not to go to the burial. They came by the house later to comfort Armontine. Keppard was clearly shaken; Jimmy again was the first... to go. According to Armontine, Keppard went to a corner and sat down and sobbed and the tears began to roll down the faces of everyone in the room.(4)

A sad event occurred later about 1933, a few musicians had just finished visiting Eddie Vincent and they were leaving. Vincent decided to go down the stairs with the guys. He lived on the third floor and he was carrying the saxophone Jimmy Palao had lent him. It slid from under his arm, in his attempt to catch it, he hit it and it seemed to propel into the air and as he reached to grab the saxophone it started falling over the banister. All the same time the other musicians were descending the steps and had reached the second floor when they heard him holler, the saxophone was falling and as they looked up they saw Eddie jump up to reach the saxophone and he fell over the banister to his death. What a tragedy! All the men kneeling around the body that now lay sprawled and broken and they were sobbing and pleading with Eddie to speak.(5)

1919 Two buddies from Algiers, Eddie Vincent and Jimmy Palao, en route to unknown destination (Family album)

Armontine "Cookie" said in 1963 thirty-eight years after her husband's death she was introduced to Modesta Palao born 2/22/1913 who said she was his daughter…and that her mother, Celestine Baptiste died in 1915 when Modesta was two years old and she never saw her father. Jimmy was on the road and although he had returned to New Orleans, he never saw the baby.(6) This was during the time that Armontine and Jimmy were separated. Jimmy never made any mention to Armontine wasn't too pleased to receive this new information. Clotilde, Jimmy's oldest daughter had heard about Modesta in 1960 and she had verified the information.

Even after the death of Jimmy Palao, he remained the love of Armontine's life. She spoke of him until her death, at the age of 104. She passed on and is buried in Chicago, Ill, St. Mary's Cemetary, located at 87th Hamlin, Evergreen Park, Il 60642. Jazz has been called "America's Classical Music" and America's only true art form. Classical music the tune is played the same each time you hear it. In Jazz the melody would not be treated the same way by any individual player. Individual creativity is encouraged, sought after, rewarded and absolutely necessary for the art of "Jazz" to survive.

Jimmy Palao when he played with The Original Creole Orchestra he and many others didn't have the advantage of recording so it was necessary to document how they came into being and their personalities, their hardships, the obstacles and opportunities they faced and the sounds and reactions to this new music known to be Jazz. A lot of time has been spent looking for just a hint of how Jimmy Palao and the Original Creole band sounded. The answer has been right under our nose. As we listen to the music of that day we hear the remnants of Jimmy Palao's Original Creole Band.

We do not hear the music that he would have recorded with the Original Creole Band but we hear the music just as he wished us to hear it … as he freely gave way to the concept of developing the free form of Jazz … that is to let others be heard and display their musical talent. It wasn't his music from his instrument that he wanted heard. He wanted us to take in the greats as their sounds developed. After all that is why Jazz... is Jazz…. We hear George Baquet April 1923 accompanying Bessie Smith on Columbia records playing the clarinet in tunes such as "Aggravatin' Papa" and "Beale Street Mama". We might hear Jimmy Palao's soulful playing of the violin on "Love Found You For Me", Freddy Keppard on cornet with Paramount Records July 1926, playing "Stockyard Strut" and "Salty Dog". Dink Johnson was the drummer for the Original Creole Band he played cornet and recorded on the Nordskog and Sunshine labels. He can be heard performing with Ory's "Sunshine Orchestra" on the old familiar tunes "Krooked Blues" and Sidney Bechet blows "Egyptian". The sounds of Jazz continue to grow and we still hear the greats...Louie Armstrong singing and playing. New Orleans Miles Davis – "Kinda Blue", John Coltrane - "My Favorite Thing", Dave Brubeck - 'Take Five" Theolodius Monk - "Reflections",

Chick Corea's - "Return to Forever", The list goes on and on... I was just about to complete my research, on the Jazz Cardinals, who Freddie Keppard featured on his records; I went to an online database and there were the listed names of Freddie Keppard's Jazz Cardinals. They were listed as follows Freddie Keppard-cornet, Eddie Vincent-trombone, Johnny Dobbs-clarinet, Arthur Campbell-piano, Jimmy Palao-violin, Jasper Taylor-wood blocks, Papa Charlie Jackson-Vocal. This of course, will require further research. Jimmy Palao loved Jazz and he wanted everyone to love Jazz so he toured taking his talented friends and Jazz to greater heights. He helped spread this art form throughout the North and Midwest.(7)

From all historical accounts it is evidenced that Jimmy Palao was the first to give Jazz its name, unless someone has information and evidence to prove otherwise. I am sure whatever spiritual zone he has entered that he is still in his renowned position of leader basking in the joy of the famous musical giants that are being heard from yesterday and today.... This is the free style of Jazz. That is what makes Jazz... Jazz. In retrospect, however, Jimmie Palao was the leader of the Original Creole Jazz Band and they were the first New Orleans band to travel extensively, sharing the gift of Jazz as they pioneered a path that would be followed by others. They were the greatest Jazz musicians of that time, The world had witnessed Jazz royalty at its best, even though James Palao and the Original Creole Orchestra made no such claim he really was the first original King of "Kings of Jazz".(8) This genius developed this style of music reflected the passion and creativity of an era.

Jimmy Palao's artistry or fine tuning of every sound from this orchestra and his desire to let the new techniques from each band member be heard changed the music landscape forever. America and the world have been profoundly affected by his originality. After the tour of the Original Creole Orchestra Jazz music swept throughout the country and gained respect as a Black American art form. For the first time in history, the culture of a minority became the desire of the majority. Jazz is the most compelling, complex and beautiful musical form of art in existence. As a musical language of communication, Jazz is the first indigenous American style to affect music in the rest of the nations. Historians, scholars, writers and intellectuals for over one hundred years have researched and substantiated the appeal of Jazz music.

As Theodore Roosevelt stated in 1905:

"The best Leader is the one who has sense enough to pick good men to do what he wants done, and self-restraint to keep from meddling with them while they do it. Jimmy Palao had done his job well.

Clotilde always felt her father was loyal to her mom. Around 1989 Clotilde shared the following story with her 101 year old mother Armontine that she had read in one of Lil Hardin books. Lil Hardin spoke well of Jimmy Palao's character in one of her excerpts from traveling on the road with her "big brothers". She said "the band members had always shown me nothing but respect…" She more or less testified to Jimmy's upstanding character she said "Jimmy Palao was an honest hard working and trustful man…"(9) Clotilde said Cookie for a moment or two said nothing, then she removed her eyeglasses and said. "Your father was a good man."

Chapter Nine

Sounds of Jazz in Memory

In picture after picture, what I felt and saw in my 'mind's eye' were people - people who lived, played music, worked hard to make a living, and had no idea they were making Jazz History. One aspect however is missing, the sounds of the bands and the people and the city. [Author unknown] The names had no sounds linked to them: this statement worried me because without sound from these recordings the music continued to flourish. How could this be? We lacked phonographs, we lacked recordings, and many people didn't have electricity! Is it that the twentieth century researcher is audio visual: and fails to realize the times were before the TV and records were not available everywhere and recording equipment was still quite expensive and not always affordable for the average consumer? Music and life didn't depend upon sounds being carried through talking machines or on phonographs. The world depended on performances, oral and visual perceptions and word of mouth and newspapers and critical interpretations from reviewers to carry this new music. People looked forward to the entertainers coming to them. They loved live performances and the shows and the new dances. They loved the human connection which gave a sense of belonging, they no reason to kvetch about being alone. They loved to dress for the times. People of yesterday carried the sounds and performances in their memory. Before the advent of recordings it was the Original Creole Orchestra that introduced this new musical form of Jazz to many cities in the USA and Canada. It was the music this band from New Orleans played that the people wanted to hear more of.

With the popularity of the phonographic record, and the demand to hear Jazz, records were being recorded. Later in the 1920s, the boom of Jazz would come into the homes thanks to the radio which dramatically accelerated that communication from region to region. Jazz was as much the product of New Orleans' melting pot as the product of an organizational and technological revolution. Also during this time the phonograph was drastically improved. This allowed the music to spread even easier as more and more people began buying phonographs and records.

Recording companies didn't always name the instrumentalist that played with the soloist and/or artist of choice. They may have just given the ensemble a group name, such as the Jazz Cardinals that played on the Keppard tunes. We searched high and low and found no such group with this name. If names were given we were unable to verify those names because they were not found as recognized musicians.

Keppard, Bill Johnson and Jimmy Palao were inseparable. They remained close friends and confidants throughout the years. I believe that when Keppard cut the records with Victor he would have only played with those musicians he was familiar with. The tunes were the same tunes played with the Original Creole Orchestra. The digitally re-engineered records allow you to clearly hear how the music and musicians in times gone by sounded.

Digital recording now provides us with clear audible snapshots of yesterday's music. You are now for the first time able to hear the masters of yesterday as they sounded in live performances. Digitally re-engineered music removes all of the crackles, pops and scratches, signs of aging or heavy use, vinyl or shellac noise, tape hissing all of the distortion is miraculously gone, replaced by pure music, in true hearing quality. You can listen for an hour, a week, the rest of your life? Technology has also provided us with open public records to explore and after extensive reading and research you can now discover the more information on the musical artist who began sharing the sounds of Jazz with the world.

We felt justified in identifying these musicians because the descriptions of how each played match the performances. You can hear in the "The One Love Belongs to Somebody Else" and "Cutie Blues" how Jimmy's violin leads with the melody and glides softly through the entire composition keeping balance to the end of the tune and he is there to bring the melody back at the conclusion. "So In the Venice" you hear the familiar slapping to the beat on the bass that only Bill Johnson was known for, and you hear the laughing of Keppard's cornet in "So This is Venice" "Scissor Grinder Joe". "Salty Dog" and "Cajun Stripper" are two renditions that sound modern almost as musicians of today would sound. Only the Keppard identifications is definite. However, after a great deal of listening and researching there is reasonable belief among many who have studied and listened to these records over and over that the violinist in the background is Jimmy Palao and the bass player slapping the bass is Bill Johnson. Even if they are not the instrumentalist these are the same tunes they played and these records are great examples how they sounded when they played with the Original Creole Orchestra. Cajun Stripper sounds pretty close to the music of today. The Original Creole Orchestra was known for its rendition of the "Egyptian" and "In Mandalay", we have not been able to local a recording of either tune...

There were other musical sounds in New Orleans. Armontine Palao always said her husband could sing very well and had he not become such a good musician, she felt the world would have loved his melodic voice.

Samuel Charters tells of a woman who moved into the Pontalba Apartments in1885 and she recalled "Every night I would see the musicians going through the streets with their guitars and they would stand under the galleries serenading. They sang sweet love songs and I could hear their wonderful voices in the quiet. The first night in New Orleans my husband and I walked through the Vieux Carre (French Quarter) together in the Moonlight. It was a beautiful spring night. When we turned the corner in front of the Cabildo, right across the street from our flat, there was a man under the arches playing a 'hurdy gurdy' (is a stringed musical instrument with a crank-turned wheel that rubs the strings. like a violin bow, sounds similar to a violin) playing very softly, 'After the ball is over… after the dance is through…"

At this point I began to wonder how we could have over-looked the Jazz vocalist in the early 1900's. Trixie Smith Singing "Messin' Around" backed by Keppard Playing cornet, Alberta Hunter's rendition of "Tain't Nobody's Biz-ness If I Do" or Bessie Smith appropriately called "the first complete "Jazz" singer" belting out "St. Louis Blues" or Mamie Smith singing "Nobody knows when you are down and out", or the harmonizing of band members. Lawrence Gushee in his book "Pioneers of Jazz" documents several complimentary news reviews, Portland, November 23: banner entertainment... The Evening Telegram;: Oregon Daily Journal :the audience couldn't get enough... after hearing the band once the audience wouldn't let it go until the band had played every number they knew... The headlines read "Creole Band makes a hit. ... Superb program Keeps Audience at Highest Pitch of Enjoyment of All Time". The review I found of most interest was the mention of the Original Creole Orchestra singing which was rarely talked about, it was in the Tacoma Monday, November 16, 1914, the Daily News and the reporter for the Daily Ledger both made similar observations.

"The seven "Creole" musicians were a riot. As a matter of fact they appear to be colored men and not Creoles, but their music hits the bulls eye and they are masters of Barber shop harmonies in their singing... the instrumental numbers have a tilt that would make a strongman want to shake his feet." Supportive evidence was found in the article "Play that Barbershop Chord: a case for the African American origin of Barbershop Harmony" by Lynn Abbott,"An interesting view of grassroots recreational quartet activity during the early 1900'scan be drawn from recollections left by New Orleans Jazz pioneers..."

Recalling his teenage years in New Orleans before World War I, trumpeter Lee Collins said: "... there used to be lots of guys around New Orleans who could sing real good. They got up quartets-my Aunt Esther's husband was the head of many a one - and would go around to some of their friends homes to sing and eat and drink beer... that was some of the most beautiful singing you would ever hope to hear." This subject alone could fill a book. I could not write this passage without mentioning the memorable and wonderful sounds of the soulful singing heard in New Orleans.

Then the sounds in memory of Hurricane Katrina in New Orleans by way of modern technology brought attention to the world of a history that was fading away. It's a city surrounded by the sounds of water -- Lake Pontchartrain, the Mississippi River, and myriad bayous, canals and waterways. New Orleans is below sea level and has a complex system of levees, drainage canals, spillways and pumping stations. The levee's were not properly repaired and gave way to the high destructive winds and torrid rains of Hurricane Katrina. A horrifying picture emerged on Television all over the world of a city drowned by the raging waters throughout New Orleans.

The devastation that New Orleans experienced from this hurricane shall never be forgotten. On August 28th, 2005, Hurricane Katrina hit the southern coast of the United States with devastating effect. There is no feasible way to comprehend or explain what anyone is feeling when loved ones are dead and all their personal possessions are destroyed. The pain is agonizing. Where has time gone? New Orleans is still under repair and in need of American support.

This city has substantiated itself. It rises and blooms again and again with the undaunted spirit of the people, through periodic floods, hurricanes and fires. It's all part of their culture and way of life if you look back at the history of the New Orleans culture; the people realized that in the midst of tragedy that they must work hard to get beyond the moment and move forward to tomorrow.

New Orleans Jazz has never seemed more important to me than it does now. Jazz, the memories and knowledge gained from the older musicians, and the strength and wisdom that comes from a life filled with music. These things will always be and will forever enrich souls. Once again, tradition gives a sense of hope and direction for the future. Though the road ahead will be difficult, as they move forward to their new beginnings in New Orleans and the sound of music in memory will continue on.

"ONCE THE SOUNDS OF JAZZ HIT THE FAN BELT IN NEW ORLEANS NOTHING COULD STOP IT!!!"

The wonderful sound of Jazz, are the sounds of the future. Jazz is amazing what sounded like extremism in improvisation years ago now those same sounds are sensible and comforting to the soul and are now masterpieces. . "Kinda Blue", Miles Davis; "My Favorite Things", John Coltrane; George Baquet; Freddie Keppard "Salty Dog" and I could go on and on.

Dedicated to the Palao Family
James "Jimmy" Palao Armontine Carter-Palao

I write this book In Memory of: the loving care and attentiveness given to me by my husband James Palao Singleton Sr. God granted all of the Palao women long lives and the moments to share this story of James "Jimmy" Palao with me so I could share his story… 86 years after his death and 102 years after he began his journey to spread Jazz and give Jazz to the world. .

James Palao's wife Armontine Carter-Palao 1885-1989 104 years
The Daughters of Armontine Palao and James Palao:
　Clotilde Palao-Wilson 1909-1995 86 years
　Mable Palao-Williams 1912-2008 94 years
　Agatha Palao-Singleton 1915-1999 84 years
　Anita Palao-McAdams 1918-1995 77 years
　The Daughter of James Palao and Celestial Baptiste
　Modesta Palao -Spooner 1913- 2009 96 years

Epilogue

Epilogues are like the roots of a tree that are always in bloom. This historical account is just the beginning of many truths to be unearthed. This is what makes Jazz... Jazz yesterday and today. Jazz is musical freedom to be heard. Wynton Marsalis refers to Jazz as "The Music of Democracy." Jazz is music of conversation, and that's what you need in a democracy. "Talk to me baby" "I hear You Talking" "Bring It On Home" "Tell It like It Is" "Keep It Real" You have to be willing to hear another person's point of view and respond to it as "Freedom of speech." This is the call and response style of Jazz". Marsalis also states; that "Jazz means learning to respect individuality and difference of opinion. You don't have to agree with me, I don't have to agree with you... it's learning how to blend and live harmoniously with differences, even when they're opposites." It is learning how to make sweet music together. This was proven when known enemies, the Onward Brass band and the Excelsior Band were recruited in the army as the Immune Ninth Infantry (as mentioned in chapter IV) to fight for a common cause and from that united front they learned to play together, a music that was still expressed individually but they learned to respect the talent of each of other as skilled musicians. They came home from the army never to fight each other again but only to share their talents with each other and the world. By 1905 Jimmie Palao had been exposed to the musical talents of many Jazz artists and him as leader and Bill Johnson as manager of the Imperial Band then formed the Original Creole Orchestra. The Original Creole Orchestra was the first to travel through 75 cities and they gained national prominence under the leadership of Jimmie Palao. The public loved their music and their sophisticated style. They left a style of music that has been talked about and captured the spirit of the world. Books are written about the Original Creole Orchestra and its leader Jimmie Palao in French and German.

I would like to thank Joan Lee who edited and put the information online I would like to thank Scott Singleton for his support and Breawnna Lee for her assistance with the short video script and documentary on Jimmy Palao. In the last two years of my research my daughter came across the name of a young lady online who said she was the granddaughter of Jimmy Palao. I did make contact with Dr. Lois Tilman and she was the daughter of Modesta Palao. She was caring for Modesta who was 94 years old and in the final years of her life. Modesta had always sought acceptance in her father's family. She and her family are now listed in their proper place in the book "Sankofa - Our Family Tree" by Joan Singleton. It is a pictorial and documented review which outlines the family ancestry, dating back to 1820. I also have communicated with her son Lester Mornay, and he has been instrumental in spreading the news about his grandfather, Jimmy Palao. I must say that even though I have known them for a short period of time. They are very loving and wonderful people.

I would like to say that my research is finally complete it has been in the making for over twenty-five years. This is the third copyright. It has grown from a 30 page essay to a novel. Once you have read this story, you will realize that it can never be said that the final page has been written. There will always be questions to be answered.. History is such a difficult subject truths are always being unearthed. These are ithe final pages of 'Keep It Real...the life story of Jimmy Palao, "The King of Jazz".

Before publishing I have allowed my work to be viewed by readers who would not normally be interested in the subject of Jazz. If these people find my account worthy of their time I will be delighted. Of course, there are those who are experts in their fields who wish to emphasize their superior knowledge on a particular facet or period. .All is acceptable for this is a research in continuous progress. I have written for the widest possible audience and included as much graphical detail as I could. I wish I were an expert on the whole of this period. The fact is that neither I nor anybody else can be completely sure of all because there is still so much be discovered.. Facts are substantiated by evidence. I write to confirm the evidence not to deny the evidence which is the obvious proof. I have allowed the story of Jimmy Palao to take its own path, not the path I wished it to take.

Let us celebrate over 100 years of Jazz ...Our Declared and Designated National Treasure to the World. "Music is the surviving link to the force of most things; it eases the pain felt by our human spirits and heightens the joyous moments of our life. As stated by Dr. Robert L. Taylor, "Jazz is America's classical music and in terms of its complexity, sophistication, versatility, and content, along with its vast range of repertoire, or any other comparative critical quality that one wishes to apply to it, the artistic, aesthetic, and developmental attributes of jazz now easily rivals in quality and substance anything that has ever come out of Europe, or anywhere else for that matter."

Everyone deserves to know the truth about this great music art form, and the major bill passed gone un-noticed by some, Resolution 57 designating Jazz as a National Treasure, introduced and written by the Honorable John Conyers Jr. was passed by the House of Representatives September 23, 1987. And it was passed by the Senate December 4, 1987. On December 4, 1987, the U.S. Senate concurred with the U.S. House of Representatives and approved Resolution 57 designating Jazz as a National Treasure

Here are excerpts from Resolution 57:

JAZZ has achieved preeminence throughout the world as an indigenous American music and art form, bringing to this country and the world a uniquely American musical synthesis and culture though the African-American experience, and makes evident to the world an outstanding artistic model of individual expression and democratic cooperation within the creative process, thus fulfilling the highest ideals and aspirations of our diverse society.

- It is a unifying force bridging cultural, religious, and ethnic and age differences in our diverse society.
- It is a true music of the people, finding its inspiration in the cultures and most personal experiences of the diverse peoples that constitute our nation,

- It has evolved into a multifaceted art form which continues to birth and nurture new stylistic idioms and culture fusions.
- It has had a historic, pervasive, and continuing influence on other genres of music both here and abroad, and become a true international language adopted by musicians around the world. Jazz as a musical language is best able to express contemporary realities from a personal perspective.
- It is in the best interest of the national welfare and all of our citizens to preserve and celebrate this unique art form.

Now, therefore, be it resolved by the House of Representatives, that it is the sense of Congress that jazz is hereby designated as a rare and valuable national American treasure; to which we should devote our attention, support, and resources; to make certain it is preserved, understood, and promulgated.

Jazz - A Valuable National American Treasure Public Law 108-72 108th Congress, 1st Session SEC.6. SENSE OF CONGRESS REGARDING JAZZ APPRECIATION MONTH: The biggest problems that Jazz has continually had to endure have been poor exposure by American educational institutions, a general lack of serious attention and interest from the public. Jazz ultimately emerges as the most vital, the most important, and the most original artistic and cultural contribution that America has ever made to the rest of the world.

"It is in the quiet crucible of our personal private sufferings that our noblest dreams are born and Gods greatest gifts are given, in compensation for what we've been through."

God's Message To All from Wintley Phipps

Bibliographical Notes

This is a listing of newspapers, books oral and written interviews by the world's foremost Jazz critics and scholars and by the individuals who took part in the development of Jazz.

The full credit for unearthing, checking and cross-checking the information about Jimmy Palao of this otherwise forgotten musician goes to those who left us with such memorable detailed information and vivid descriptions of this one man, times and music. The information, however, is spread out over many different publications and is for the first time collected together in chronological and numerical sequence for easy access, compiled from the sources as cited. There is only historical purpose involved with the presentation of this revealing novel. Please note, however, that the collective and combined works of all researchers should be made available to new researchers who then can start their research on a sound reliable basis.

The other day I read the Swing/Jazz age is returning! We can look forward to good times with fabulous shows, incredible live music, and dancing competitions and much, much more! I believe everyone should know how it all began. So enjoy, Keep It Real! The story of Jimmy Palao captures the magic of the Jazz Era at its peak.

The reference notes give a source of citations and it would become redundant to state them here. The following list of collections and articles provide suggestions for collateral reading germane to this story. In order to piece together the life of Jimmy Palao, I compiled facts from many accounts in over 250 books. The images displayed throughout this historical account have been obtained from The J. Singleton Family album, Sankofa, Our Family Tree, and by J. Singleton, University of Chicago, Louisiana University and other educational institutions, the staff from Tinley Park, IL Public Library, 1890,1900,1910 and the 1920 Census and Baptismal records and interviews.. The information can be found in the following collections;

1. The André Chaves Collection in UCLA Approx. 1150 books, including reference works (discographies, catalogs, guides, etc.); monographs on musicians, styles, institutions, places; jazz histories; literature with jazz themes; photographs. This collection forms the core of a research-oriented non-circulating Jazz Reference collection.

2. William Russell Jazz Collection in The Williams Research Center of the Historic New Orleans Collection, 410 Chartres Street New Orleans, LA 70130, 42,500 items 1830-1992 Sept. 12 Bulk dates 1930-1950 William Russell, born Russell William Wagner (1905-1992), was a jazz historian and collector who focused on traditional New Orleans style Jazz. The William Russell Jazz Collection documents his lifetime of studying New Orleans Jazz and related musical forms such as brass bands, ragtime, and gospel music. Mr. Russell amassed an extensive collection of jazz memorabilia including musical instruments, records, piano rolls, sheet music, photographs, books and periodicals. His collection traces the development of Jazz in New Orleans and follows the movement of musicians to New York, Chicago, California, and beyond. It encompasses notes from Mr. Russell's research, audiotapes, programs, posters, correspondence, films, business cards, notes, clippings, and scrapbooks

3. The Al Rose Collection includes hundreds of old Jazz photographs, many that were used in conjunction with Rose's publication, New Orleans Jazz: A family Album. The works of several distinguished contemporary photographers such as celebrated art photographer Lee Friedlander, and reputed amateur Jazz photographer Dr. Bernard Steinau are featured.

4. The Rutgers Collections is the largest archive of Jazz and Jazz related materials in the world.. A collection of more than 30,000 photographs taken over nine decades serve as an internationally consulted resource of images for publications and broadcast documentaries. A collection of oral history materials, most notably the Jazz Oral History Project of the National Endowment for the Arts (NEA) which was transferred to the Institute in 1979. The collection of some 6000 books includes practically every book published on Jazz, including rare early works.

5. Hogan Jazz Archive, Tulane University. The Hogan Jazz Archive, a department within Tulane University's Special Collections Division, is a renowned resource for New Orleans Jazz research. The collection includes oral histories, recorded music, photographs and film, and sheet music and orchestrations. There are also files of manuscripts, clippings, and bibliographic references.

You will find excerpts from the interviews of Armontine Palao-Dorsey and Clotilde Palao-Glover Interview, Translated Notes of Clotilde Glover. Peter Bocage, – Interview, (WR Collection,) Ed Dawson – Interview Pops Foster; Robert Goffin Ed "Montudi" Garland –Interview, Paul Howard – Interview, Bill Johnson, – Interview, Dink Johnson, Charles Love, Charles – Interview, (WR Collection), Manetta, Manuel – Interview, (WR Collection) Josh Porterfield (Reel V), Al Rose, John Underwood, William Russell, – Interview, and two anonymous donors, due to personal issues, wish to remain anonymous. Credit is attributed in the work when known. Unless otherwise credited, the works and information and illustrations are in the public domain, based on current U.S. and international copyright acts and were issued for publication over 75-100 years ago.

My trunks have literally detonated on their own with the gatherings of collected information and research, which I have finally given life to and placed in order, to give a clear picture of the life of the most important band leader of this era. I found it necessary to include the tell all's; which led to the career path he took, his childhood memories, his relationships to family, friends and band members. New information and insight into the scope and importance of American Jazz History is ongoing..." All material appearing in this book are in the public domain. Public domain information allows the free exchange of knowledge, which is meant to allow everyone the equal opportunity to be heard, to view, critique, or otherwise examine the works of mankind. It is requested that in any subsequent use of the expressions from this work, the author be given appropriate acknowledgment. Please note, however, that the collective and combined works of all researchers have been made available to new researchers who then can start their research on a sound reliable basis

Some people like to wait for things to happen! Some people like to prevent things from happening! Some people like to make things happen! Let us begin the Celebration of over 100 years of Jazz!!! America's National Treasure

*There are pictures; each one is significant in telling the Jazz story of James "Jimmie" Palao. They can be found at the Chicago Historical Society in Chicago. Also his first instruments can be found at the Chicago Historical Society.

*There are reels of interviews found in the Historic New Orleans Collection. A personal history of the development of Jazz in New Orleans unfolds in the many reels of interviews

Appendix 1

Statement and Findings

Findings based on most relevant historical accounts
to Statements 1-15, in question.

Researchers and historians are still learning about Jazz history. Historical findings will be a work in progress for many years to come; there are many observations and theories and various opinions based upon factual findings about what is important and what really happened in the history of Jazz. Most Jazz history dates back to 1914. I am going to take you back a little further, to 1900.

I don't wish in any way to discount or diminish the words of the Jazz historians or the oral interview of the musicians of the early 1900's. They have kept Jazz alive and offered treasured memories from the past. They told what they saw and experienced as they understood and/or remembered the beginning moments of Jazz which I have thoroughly inspected and investigated.

The following information is stated to clarify the most relevant findings according to logical interpretation of events according to the history of the times and circumstances. The Census records and the oral histories provide us with definite details from the past. The photographs serve as evidence and corrections to any misinterpretations. Most of the information is recorded and dates back more than 80 years ago and is considered in public domain.

1. Statement: Jimmie Palao was the originator of the word "Jazz"

Findings

1. Jimmie Palao called this music "Jazz" and no other musician is given the credit for having an earlier first mention of the term "Jaz". Jazz is found on his business card, as early as 1908, [Jazz, A History Of Jazz : the New York Scene]. Al Rose gave Clotilde Palao Wilson a copy of her father Jimmy Palao's 1908 business card, [Al Rose Collection}.

2. Jimmie Palao's wife Armontine said he always referred to the music he played as Jazz from the time she met him in 1905. [, Armontine Palao's Interview]. Pg 62

3. Throughout all of my research no other musician of this time is found in every major band except Jimmie Palao. Jazz was spread through traveling and the word Jazz itself was spread the same way. It is evident that through his extensive travels and from his musical contacts he had greater access to circulate his business card and spreading the word "Jazz", more so than the average musician. There are constant historical accounts of friendships developed, Freddie Keppard, Eddie Vincent, Pops Foster,[Pops Foster;], Ed (Red) Garland, he grew up with Victor and Manuel Manetta and Eddie Duson *[WR Collection]*. As a friendly gesture he lent his saxophone to Eddie Vincent. He had a real quiet sweet personality and a catchy way of talking, better known to us as Jazz Slang. He taught Buddy Bolden how to play his instrument. Jimmie Palao played his violin high so that Freddie Keppard could hear the melody because Keppard couldn't read music. This allowed Keppard to improvise upon the tune. This was Palao's best kept secret. It was evident that Jimmie Palao was well liked among his fellow musicians and he certainly influenced others. The one copy of music we found is devoted to his friend George Baquet, dated Dec 11, 1911. According to the Gushee interview with Armontine Palao, there is more music. Jimmy Palao played with all the "Top Cats". According to historical accounts

[Combo USA] he played two and three gigs a day and set in with many groups. He also played vaudeville and in marching bands.

Business card dated on back 1908 #1 Leader of Original Creole Band Card supplied by Al Rose

4. I also found that from the earliest mention of the term 'Jazz' that Jimmy Palao was always present in that band when the term was used. All of this information adds to the evidence that James Palao was the first to use the word "Jaz" to describe the music that comes from New Orleans. There is another business card in evidence for 1914. It has been said that the first mention of Jazz in 1914 was in Chicago and California. Jimmy Palao was playing a gig in Chicago in 1914 and in Los Angeles and San Francisco in 1914.

5. Another theory is that he used the phrase Jaz. as a term for his name Jas. This is not a likely theory because the Card with Jaz written several times has his name spelled as Jas.

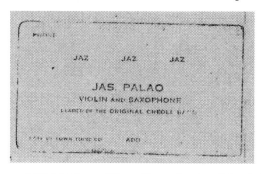

Business card 1914 #2 Late of Town Topics-Leader of Creole Band >>

2. <u>Statement</u> The Imperial Band was in uniform and then suits

Findings

1. Trend setters. According to Johnny St Cyr "we had no special uniforms for dance band work, just regular suits. Around 1907 the parade bands all got uniforms. They were known as the band in blue – the boys in brown, etc...

1905, The Imperial Band　　　　　*1905, The Imperial Band*

3. <u>Statement</u> Creole is written on this card

<u>Findings</u>

1. This explains why the Jimmy Palao's business card states Creole. It was a selling point because Creole musicians were in high demand in Los Angeles, Chicago, New York because of their reading skills and/or ability to play New Orleans Jazz...

Business card 1917-1918 #3Creole Palao and Jimmy Palao spelled out evidence of violin, tenor Saxophone, Tenor Banjo

4. <u>Statements</u>: Original Creole Band founded 1908

<u>Findings</u>

1. It is recorded that Bassist Bill Johnson and Jimmy Palao founded the band in June 1904 and afterwards added a cornet player, Ernest Coycault and a trombonist. They left New Orleans to tour the Southwest with the Town Topics. The group settled in Los Angeles for a time and for a while its pianist was Dink Johnson. Bill Johnson went on to Los Angeles to set up gigs for the band where they decided to settle.

2. Baquet gave 1908 as the date that the group, organized by Johnson, with the leader being Jimmy Palao left New Orleans; Baquet also stated that the orchestra traveled on "a hustlin trip all over Dixie, making money as they barnstormed, just like the German bands used to do at that time."(Ramsey 1941). Pg 60 /VI).

3. The first New Orleans band to play the New York theaters was a six piece band lead by Jimmy Palao which coincides with the date on his second business card year dated 1908. [J. Singleton] The Creole band opened in a show called the Town Topics at the Winter Garden Theatre 1908 (Jazz A History of Jazz). The band was organized by a Bass player named Bill Johnson who had moved to Los Angeles in 1909 to establish his home base as California.

4. According to Armontine Palao, Bill Johnson didn't always travel or play with the band. He would scout out the locations and travel ahead to set appointments and arrange the stage settings. Her husband Jimmie Palao as leader never missed a gig or set.

5. According to an account that traces the life of Jimmy Palao that was written in French and later translated in English, "When Jimmy Palao arrived in Los Angeles and it was he who begin to organize the Original Creole Orchestra and he

sent telegrams to Baquet, Vincent, Keppard and Norwood Williams." (La Nouvelle-Orleans Capitale Du Jazz)

5. Statement: The photograph of The Original Creole Orchestra was published in 1909.

Findings:

1. Time date of picture of Original Creole Jazz Band taken in late 1909 or early 1910 in California. One source stated that Zue Robertson was asked to join the band and for some reason he didn't. The entire line up as in the picture went, Freddie Keppard, Eddie Vincent, Bill Johnson, Dink Johnson, George Baquet and Jimmy Palao and W. M Johnson [William Russell Reel III [of 4] Sept. 4. 1962]. Bill Johnson and the whole Creole Band left New Orleans in 1911, they were in Los Angeles in 1911 [William Russell interview with Bill Johnson,WRC] The Creole Band opened in Chicago Dec. 1911 Shows Bill Johnson as manager and James Palao as leader. (Chicago Defender). (Jazzmen)

2. Furthermore, the Poster and the photograph of the Original Creole Orchestra given by Bill Johnson to Bill Russell, was reproduced in *Jazzmen* (Ramsey and Smith 1939, between pp. 32 and 33), clearly point to the Creole band organized for providing dance music, which obviously took place between Palao's arrival in the latter part of 1913 and the Cross/ Rivers boxing match in August 1914 (I really don't know why the Chicago Defenders article dated 1911 along with the poster information is ignored by Jazz scholars. This proves that the picture was in existence in 1911 and these band member united before the picture was taken which gives evidence to Armontine's account that the picture was taken in or about 1909. (The original picture in the first edition of Jazzmen shows this as a poster.)

3. Sometimes information is omitted that is clearly obvious. (It reminds me of a picture taken in one of the classiest books recently published with the large picture that names

James Palao as the leader of the band yet the author is so taken with his own interpretation that he names the leader as Freddie Keppard.)

4. We are lucky indeed that such firmly dated evidence survives.

5. The Original Creole Orchestra played the New York theaters in a show called the Town Topics. (business card names Jimmie Palao as band leader and violinist) Picture taken in 1909 of Original Creole band. [Jazz: A History Of Jazz: The New York Scene, Edited by Samuel charters] (Pgs 54-57) According to Al Rose, "The first New Orleans Jazz group to appear in the North, also played in 1911 for the first time in Chicago at the Grand Theater." Picture from Chicago defender evidence of this names Jimmy Palao as Leader, violinist and Bill Johnson as Manager and bass player (Jazzmen, edited by Frederick Ramsey, Jr, and Charles Smith).

Tuxedo s tyle 1890-1925   *Tuxedo with white tie and*   *1903*
                            white shirt worn 1880-
                            1920 Picture taken 1909

6. Statement: Concerning Keppards decision to not record. It was the bands decision along with Keppard to not record. The final decision would be left up to the Manager Bill Johnson and the Leader Jimmy Palao.

Findings

1. Discovered all recording would lack quality because the 78 record recording time was 10-12 minutes, this would not give enough time for the melody and the improvisation to be played through.

2. Also researched Victor, there is no record of an offer being made this early (1915) to record Black Americans music. Either the representative was in disguise and was a song shark or Keppard simply told the story, to make himself seem important, because all transactions for the Creole band were handled and or arranged by Bill Johnson.

3. Found there was a record made by the Creole Band under the name Bill Johnson which makes sense because he was the only one who would arrange a recording for the Original Creole Orchestra/Band. The record was never issued; this information begins to give credence to Armontine Palao's insistence that there were at least three recordings made in 1918. This one was discovered by a British Jazz scholar. The title was "Tack Em Down", page 140. This is believed to be the first music recorded by a Black American Band. Recordings of most Black American music were in the 1920's and categorized under "Race records". Everything that Armontine has said so far has been accurate so we are still in search of two more recordings.

4. I was going over reels from the William Russell Collection interview with Bill Johnson and found the following overlooked statement; Bill Johnson had an interview with William Russell 12/19/1938 Bill Johnson mentions; that possibly another record offer was made to him by Victor. He says it came through Will Vodery. He was a leading Negro arranger in Chicago. In the interview he states that, "Will Vodery could be found c/o Handy Music Company." (William Russell Collection interview with Bill Johnson Reel #). This is the first reference I have found to a representative's name and to any contact being made

with Bill Johnson... Bill Russell lived 100 years and it seems there were very few if any other interviews done with him. I and another scholar concluded that " Vodery might have learned of the opportunity for a Black touring orchestra to make a record for Victor, and passed on the opportunity to Johnson." perhaps that started the conversation between Keppard and all of the band members that states they were against recording. It makes better sense because Bill Johnson was the manager of the band and would have been the only one to handle all business matters transactions. (I can't help but comment on the interesting background of William H. Vodrey even though he is seldom mentioned he was one of the most respected, well-known, and best-connected Black musician, conductor, director and composer in early twentieth-century America. Vodery's association with Bert Williams also led to his most prestigious job—as music supervisor of Broadway's famous annual *Ziegfeld Follies*. When Bert Williams began his tenure as a star of the *Follies,* he brought with him the Vodery orchestrations of the music for his spot on the bill. Take a moment and look him up. (1884-1951)

7. Statement: Palao's Association with A. J. Piron

Findings

1. This picture was a surprise. A picture of the AJ. Piron' Orchestra was provided by Modesta Palao and Lois Tilman. She said the saxophone player was Jimmy Palao. Jimmy did play the saxophone during this time. I was unable to locate any evidence of Jimmy Palao playing in the A.J. Piron Band for any length of time. I only found one mention of him sitting in for Piron. If anyone can bring light to this it would be appreciated... Johnny St Cyr in his interview provided evidence that Jimmie Palao played with the Olympian Band when Piron set on his violin and broke it.

2. St Cyr's account was detailed, he stated that, "One night at Economy Hall, Piron went down on the floor during intermission to talk to a girl he knew. Freddie Keppard hollered to him, "Come on man, we've got to play some music." Piron called back, "Don't yell at me, man." Piron got real hot about this and he put his violin on his chair and refused to play. During the course of the number, he forgot his violin was on the chair, and he sat on it. The members of the band laughed so hard, he packed up and went home. That was the last time he played with the Olympia Band — Jimmy Palao took his place."

8. Statement: There were three Creole Bands. Many Bands used Creole in their title

Findings

1. There was only one Original Creole Orchestra/Band which featured no stars name- The reason was that the style of Jazz was that each player was a "star". The leader of the band was Jimmy Palao and the Manager was William Manuel Johnson Keppard was never leader of Original Creole band, he was the star player. King Oliver didn't play with the Original Creole Band.

2. The Lawrence Duhe New Orleans Creole Jazz Band (1919) had the honor of leading the first Jazz Band to play at the World Series game of 1919. Members of the band were Jimmy Palao-saxophone, George field-trombone, Joe Oliver-trumpeter, Willie Humphrey- clarinet, Emmett Scott-banjo, Wellman Braux-bass player and Minor Hall-drums (Louisiana Life Series: No 3 Second Line, Jazzmen of Southwest Louisiana, 1900-1950 by Austin Sonnier Jr.). In 1920 the once Lawrence Duhe band was renamed the King Oliver Creole Band and they traveled from Chicago to San Francisco May 1921. They contracted to play with the Pergola Dancing Pavillion of San Francisco. They were a seven piece orchestra consisting of Joe Oliver, Honore

Dutrey, John Dobbs, Lillian Hardin, Minor Hall, Edward "Montudi" Garland and Jimmy Palao. The contract read as follows "…band shall play continuous dance music as played in so called nickel dances as directed by the party of the first part, between 8p.m. and 12 p.m." The contract covered a six month period extending from June to December (Jazzmen edited by Frederick Ramsey).

3. Joe Oliver took leadership of the Lawrence Duhe Band in 1920 in Chicago and renamed the Band the King Joe Oliver Creole Band.

9. Statement:. Jimmie Palao Great violin player

Findings:

1. According to Lil Hardin, "A typical inclusion was Jimmy Palao's violin. Palao was more than the fiddler of a polite string trio. He too could go back into the alley" His fiddle also served a secret face-saving function. For Keppard alone of the group could not read music. But he could pick up from the most complex melodies and harmonies with one hearing. So Palao played the melody straight all of the time, up very high. If Keppard got lost in a new tune, there it was up over his head soft and clear. Technically apart from reading. Keppard was a real virtuoso."[Combo: USA: Eight Lives in Jazz by Bill Russell 1905 (pages 38-43)]

2. Lil Hardin spoke of band "I had a fit. I had never heard a band like that: They made goose pimples break out all over me. I am telling you they played loud and long and got the biggest kick out of the fit I was having over their music… The band was a sensation from the first night at the Deluxe Café, so much so that there were no available seats after 9PM and a line waiting outside that kept King Jones yelling to the high heavens that soon there would be seats…" Sugar Johnny played a growling cornet style using cups and old hats to make all kinds of funny noises. Dewey's clarinet

squeaked and rasped with his uneven scales and trills, Roy was sliding back and forth on the trombone, making a growling accompaniment to Sugar's breaks. Jimmy's violin sighed and wheezed while he scratched the strings with his bow. To top all this, Montudi, Tubby and I beat out a background rhythm that put the Bechuana tribes of Africa to shame. This was New Orleans Jazz and the people ate it up." ['Hear Me Talkin' To Ya': The Story Of Jazz By The Men Who Made It. Edited by Nat Shapiro and Nat Hentoff (pgs 91-93)]

3. Eddie Dawson (pg13) Reel III-Digest—Retyped, June 28. 1961. In Ed's opinion, the best violinist was Jimmy Palao: Manuel Manetta was second: Peter Bocage was third ; Valteau [spelling?] was next, then Tinette (spelling?) (William Russell Collection)

4. Charles Love Reel I- Summary Retyped January 16, 1960 9pg 2-3) The first band Love remembers leaving here and going North was Eddie Vincent and Jimmie Palao… "Jimmy Palao also played mellophone in the Pacific Brass band. Palao was a first class violin and mellophone player. They tell me after he left he learned how to play the saxophone…"

5. Armontine Palao speaks quite frequently about how beautiful her husband Jimmie Palao played the violin and the saxophone. I found the above statements and many more that testified to how well Jimmy played, though there were many more references to Jimmy Palao's great playing ability.

10. Statement: Jimmy Palao Played with Sophie Tucker

I really was not sure if Sophie Tucker was on the same circuit with Jimmie Palao or if he played in the band with Sophie Tucker singing or if Sophie Tucker was just one of his regular audience members. I only found two references that seem to connect him with Sophie Tucker.

Findings:

1. This first statement seems to state that "…the band members played with Sophie Tucker.… Jasper Van Pelt, trombonist… as part of Town Topics revue in 1916 where they were billed as The Five Rubes. …… Howard was in the Orpheum Theatre when Sophie Tucker sang "Some of These Days", with George Baquet, Bill Johnson, Dink Johnson, and Jimmy Palao." This was not definite I only found one such reference and nothing else to substantiate this finding, so I didn't use this information in the book. However, don't dismiss the thought there may be a source that will proof this information to be true…

2. The second statement only states that Sophie was in the audience… This information was used in the book. I found this in several sources: the most important came from Lil Hardin autobiography it read, "Lil Hardin-Armstrong's career in Jazz extended more than fifty years and centered in Chicago and New York. She got her first playing jobs through contacts made at Jones's Music Store. Her first major band experience was with the Original New Orleans Creole Jazz Band, playing at the DeLuxe Cafe. The band included Lawrence Duhé on clarinet, Sugar Johnson and Freddie Keppard on cornets, Roy Palmer on_trombone, Sidney Bechet on clarinet and soprano saxophone, Tubby Hall on drums, Jimmy Palao on violin, Bob Frank on piccolo, and Wellman Braud on bass. The Original New Orleans Creole Jazz Band played in a pure, swinging New Orleans style and was quite successful. The audience frequently contained some of the leading musicians and stars of the day, including Bill "Bojangles" Robinson, the vaudeville team of Walker and Williams, Eddie Cantor, Al Jolson, and Sophie Tucker".

11. Statement: Jimmy Palao played with Lil Hardin in Lawrence Duhe Band 1917 and in Clarence Jones Band 1919.

Findings

1. Jimmy Palao with Lil Hardin: In the issue of December 27, 1919, The Chicago whip published a photograph of a nine piece orchestra, Jones Dreamland Band. "The Jolly Jazzing Jeopards." In an Associated article, the band is further identified as Clarence Jones's but under the leaderships of "Senor E.S. Washington". Be that as you may, Lil Hardin (not yet married) is at the piano and Jimmy Palao is standing in front with a tenor sax. This is hardly visible in the Whip's halftone but amply clear in the large format print by Lil to John Steiner ad now held at the University of Chicago. She dated the photo as 1921.which I found the date to be accurate. The university gave me permission to use the photo, but due to an overload I haven't had the opportunity to go there. The one I provide from our family album isn't as clear as the one they have.

12.Statement; It was believed that many of the Musicians life style brought on early death due to drugs, drinking disease and unsanitary housing conditions and improper clothing for the extreme weather conditions,

Findings

1. By the turn of the century the AMU (American Music Union) was providing sizeable death grants to its members. At the time it was said that 40% of musicians suffered premature death from TB brought on by poor working conditions. The union also offered instrument insurance.

2. Tuberculosis was responsible for many deaths during the early 1900's. Some patients died quickly or lingered as invalids for years; some recovered, but no one could determine, when or if the disease would strike again

13. Statement: Jimmy Palao was leader of the Creole Orchestra Keppard was not leader of the Original Creole Orchestra. Nor was Johnson leader of the Creole Orchestra.

Findings:

1. It was easy to understand the source of confusion. Freddie Keppard was the star soloist in the band and he was featured nightly. So the referral to it being the Freddie Keppard Band was understandable. The public and sometimes reviewers often will mistake the "star" of the band to be the leader.

2. William Manuel Johnson was manager of the band and he arranged all the gigs, consequently no booking or business decisions were made without him. He was not always with the band, often he was scouting for other gigs. His home base was in California and he made a lot of arrangements from that location. Consequently all of the documents and business transactions were under the name of Bill Johnson including the first record cut by a Black band "Tack Em Down" registered by Bill Johnson. Also going only on historical written records one might see Bill Johnson name signed for all events and business matters pertaining to the Original Creole Orchestra and or Band.

3. Jimmy Palao was the leader. As leader of the band he did the hard work; he chose the musicians and the music, rearranged composition, developed the style of Jazz, worked and traveled with the musicians and directed the band. He was with them for every performance. He developed what will always be remembered as the first greatest musical organization in history. The Original Creole Orchestra disbanded in 1918. Jazz scholars have confirmed in book after book that Jimmy Palao was the leader of the Original Creole Orchestra.

14. Statement: It was thought that the Original Creole Orchestra Jazzmen left the Band in 1917. This was not exactly the case… Lil Hardin played

piano with The Lawrence Duhe Band which was an ensemble band. Quite often in historical accounts you will find a musician listed in two separate bands. How can one musicians or band be in two places at the same time?

Findings

1. After sorting through many of the musicians lives. There were many accounts of afterhours doubling or doubling in-between bookings... I finally went over the itinerary of the Original Creole Band and there was the answer. The solution is simple a musician or sometimes an entire band worked at both places – either in between bookings or as a fill in.

2. In 1917 Jimmy Palao played with both bands Lawrence Duhe and Original Creole Orchestra. It was not unusual for band members to play with other bands. Sometimes they had their own bands and played with other bands or on the bandstands with other bands. It was all about keeping a steady income and sometimes a lucrative income. In 1917 the Original Creole Orchestra had no bookings Mid May to Mid October, (see Appendix 29-30 – Itinerary) those members played with Lawrence Duhe Band. It was interesting to discover Lawrence Duhé and his pianist, (Lil Hardin); toured as an ensemble. The New Orleans Creole Jazz Band, (Jimmy Palao,) played in-between bookings, in mid May 1917 to mid October 1917. The Lawrence Duhe Band along with Lil Hardin consisted of various Jazz bands and /or Jazz band members through, 1917-21. This was the only band that we know of that continuously hired band members. According to Sidney Bechet the concept was different and the Lawrence Duhe Band was pretty successful and seemly drew the top stars.

15. Statement, The Original Creole Orchestra and the King Joe Oliver Creole Band are one and the same. This is not true.

Findings

1. The King Joe Oliver band didn't come into existence until late 1920 to early 1921 and should not be confused with the Original Creole Orchestra/Band.

2. Oliver attempted to join The Original Creole Orchestra in 1914 after winning a cutting contest from Keppard. Keppard was kept on with The Original Creole Orchestra. Oliver was not happy with the decision. After The Original Creole Orchestra disbanded in 1918.Jimmy Palao joined The Lawrence Duhe Band. He was with the Lawrence Duhe Band when the Band played at the Chicago White Sox game in Cominsky Park. . In 1920 Joe Oliver joined and took over leadership of The Lawrence Duhe Band and he asked Keppard to stay. Keppard left The Lawrence Duhe Band. Oliver and Sidney Becket had a terrible argument and Becket was never able to talk with any warmth toward Oliver. Oliver then renamed The Lawrence Duhe Band - The King Oliver Creole Band This was the first time Jimmy Palao played in the same band with Joe Oliver. Bill Johnson went to California and was approached with a significant contract and he called the King Oliver Band to California. Jimmy Palao and Joe Oliver were not... a match made in heaven and Oliver after a major dispute let Jimmy go. Minor Hall also left. King Joe Oliver later in 1922 selected other band members and took the band to Chicago. After several negative comments about them not being Creole, Joe Oliver later named the band "King Joe Oliver and his Dixie Syncopator's.

16. Statement: Jimmy Palao taught Buddy Bolden how to read music.

Findings:

1. Jimmy as a child traveled along the countryside with his father and they would visit with families. He met and knew

many of the children in these communities. Jimmy and his father would always return home with baskets of fruit. As Jimmy grew older he would go visit along the countryside and teach them how to set up bands and read music. Buddy Bolden was one of his students. It was said that Buddy later practiced on his instrument 24-7 and became known as the "King of the cornet" and the "Father of Jazz". Jimmy Palao later played in the Buddy Bolden Band and the teacher learned from the student. He was impressed by the style Buddy had created. Buddy became ill and never played again after 1907. Jimmy took leadership of the Imperial Orchestra and took this style of music that Buddy Bolden played. William Johnson served as the manager for the Imperial band and they were in demand. It was said with this band he began calling the music Jazz. He and William Johnson formed a partnership in 1908. Jimmy Palao gathered his friends and formed the Original Creole Orchestra and they traveled with this style of music he called Jazz…as Jazz gained national prominence.

NOTES

It seems that Jimmy Palao was at the center of most first in the history of Jazz. It is believed he was the first to coin the term Jazz, as evidenced on his business card. His band was the first to introduce collective improvisation; featuring the technical skills mastered by each of the band members. His Band was the first Black American Orchestra to travel the Vaudeville Circuits. His Orchestra was the first to travel extensively and spread Jazz throughout 75 cities in the U.S. and in Canadian cites. His band was the first Black band to join and travel the vaudeville circuits. He was one of the participants' who helped choose the first successful African American female Jazz artist, Lil Hardin.

Let it also be noted that even without recordings the names of each of the members of the Original Creole Orchestra are known. They had definitely made their mark. Bet you don't know the names, of even one of the white band members from the Original Dixieland Band, who are thought to be the first to have recordings that were published and distributed in 1917. Interesting isn't it… and leads me to believe they didn't play Jazz as it was meant to be played; that would make the first records that feature collective improvisation, to still be recognized as the first real Jazz records…

Ragtime: an encyclopedia, discography, and sheetography By David A. Jasen
"O You Sweet Rag" by James Palao
Registered E unpublished BO1875
July 9, 1941 Copyright 1917
The Publisher H. Kirkus Dugdale of Washington DC was in effect a vanity publisher, responsible for an enormous number of copyrights around this time. Although he probably deserves the derogatory epithet song shark "it is possible that in 1911 New Orleans an African America would have found it extremely difficult to be published by one of the music houses. Remarkably we find records that the composition "O You Sweet Rag" by Jimmy Palao published in 1911. (Werlein for example)

Time Line

Buddy Johnson Band [Palao, Leader.] [1895-1897
Pacific Brass Band [1897-1898]
Henry Allen Brass Band [1897-1900]
Jimmy Palao Band [Palao, Leader] [1900]
Buddy Bolden Band [1903-1905]
Imperial Jazz Band, [Palao, Leader] [1905-1907]
Olympian Band [1909]
Original Creole Jazz Band [Palao, Leader] [1908-1918]

Original Creole Orchestra Itinerary **1907-1918**
**The activities of the band during 1907 to 1913 are a little sketchy.
Approximately 80 percent of the Creole Band's time between August
1914 and April 1918 can be accounted for. This itinerary should be
helpful for following the appearances of the band I can only give
you the dates. If you ever want to read a entire coverage of the
performance. Pioneers of Jazz by Lawrence Gushee will take you
step by step through most of the listed dates. It is readers must.**

Original Creole Orchestra Itinerary - 1907 July- December
V= Variety F= Indianapolis Freeman, B= Billboard, D= Chicago
Defender

Changes in Personnel- Creole Band
William Tounsil, mandolin - Bill Johnson, guitar - Alphonse Fergend,
bass - Charley Henderson, banjo - John Collins, trumpet

July
2 New Orleans- Tom Anderson
9 Waco
16 Houston
23 Dallas Changes in Personnel
30 Ernest Coycault, trumpet- Albert Paddio, trombone [Stoddard –
1982 Reb Spikes]
August
13 Yuma
20 California
2 Los Angeles, California Red Feather

Original Creole Orchestra Itinerary – 1908
V= Variety F= Indianapolis Freeman, B= Billboard, D= Chicago
Defender

Changes in Personnel Original Creole Orchestra-1908
Jimmie Palao, leader-violin - Freddie Keppard, cornet-Danny Lewis-
double bass (1908) / Bill Johnson, Manager (1908)-double bass- (bass
Replacement 1909) Eddie Vincent, -Dink Johnson, Drums (Added
1909)-W.M. Williams or Norwood, "Gigi" Williams, George Baquet,
(Picture taken 1909

December
2 Los Angeles, California - Dreamland Tower and Lagoon, at 8th and
Spring St
January
6 California –Picture - Barbary Coast in San Francisco, California
September
3 Town Topics took them to New York, N.Y. to Chicago- California
and back to New Orleans [7-pg86

October
1 Dixie Tour

Original Creole Orchestra Itinerary - 1909-1913

V= Variety F= Indianapolis Freeman, B= Billboard, D= Chicago Defender

Very little information found on appearances the mainstream white theatrical press and the media did not work the black vaudeville circuits and consisted of very few listings of their forthcoming appearances.
January 1909
6 California –1909 Original Creole Orchestra Picture Taken
January 1911
3 Chicago, Illinois Grand Theater 1911
April 1913
13 Tuxedo Hall Easter Sunday Massacre 1913 (New Orleans)
Jimmy arrived in LA 1913

Original Creole Orchestra Itinerary – 1914, July – December
V= Variety F= Indianapolis Freeman, B= Billboard, D= Chicago Defender

January
5 Los Angeles, - Blanchard Hall
16 Hotel Alexandria
April
3 Los Angeles California - Merritt Jones Hotel, Ocean Park
May 7/1914 Baquet remembered received telegram on this day
July 11, 1914 Cross- Rivers fight
August
11 Leach-Cross fight
17 LosAngeles, Pantages Theater
24 [San Francisco, California - Oakland Theater d]
31 San Francisco, California - Pantages Theater
September
21 Winnipeg, Canada Pantage Theater s
28 Edmonton, Canada - Pantages Theater
October
5 Calgary,Canada - Pantages Theater
12 Great Falls, Montana - Pantages Theater
19 Spokane, Washington - Pantages Theater

26 Seattle, Washington - Pantages Theater
November
2 Vancouver, Canada Pantages Theater
9 Victoria, Canada Pantages Theater
16 Tacoma, Washington - Pantages Theater
23 Portland, Oregon- Pantages Theater trip made by ocean vessel to San Francisco
30 [en route?] Pantages
December
7 San Francisco, Theater Pantages
14 Oakland, Pantages Theater return engagement performed two weeks
21 [Los Angeles, California] Pantages Theater
28 San Diego, California Pantages Theater (received encores

Original Creole Orchestra Itinerary – 1915; January–June
V= Variety F= Indianapolis Freeman, B= Billboard, D= Chicago Defender

January
4 Salt Lake City, Utah
11 Salt Lake City, Utah
18 Salt Lake City, Utah
February
1 Chicago, Illinois Grand Theatre
8 Chicago, IllinoisGrand Theatre
March
8 Battle Creek, Michigan Bijou Theater
15 Ann Arbor,Michigan Majestic Theater
May
10 Chicago, Illinois - Wilson Avenue Theater (One of best playing vaudeville houses in the country) that attracted top acts Kedzie Theater
17 Champaign, Illinois Orpheum Theater
24 St. Louis, Missouri Empress Theater
June
21 St. Louis, Missouri Mannion'Park

July
5 St. Louis, Missouri Hamilton Theater
August
16 Davenport, Iowa
23 Terre Haute, Indiana, - Hippodrome Theater
30 Springfield, Illinois, - Majestic Theater – Decatur, Illinois , Empress Theater
September
6 Chicago, Illinois - American Theater – Windsor Theater
13 Racine, Wisconsin Orpheum Theater - Peoria, Orpheum
20 Bloomington, Illinois - Majestic Theater
27 St. Louis, Missouri - Theater Empress Theater- Quincy, Illinois Orpheum Theater
October
4 Galesburg, Illinois - Gaiety Theater - Galesburg, Gaiety Theater
11 Chicago, Lincoln - Theater Lacrosse, Wisconsin Opera House
18 Rock Island, Illinois - Empire Theater- Cedar Rapids
25 Waterloo. Iowa - Sioux City, Iowa - Orpheum Theater
November
1 Omaha, Nebraska - Empress Theater
8 Cedar Rapids, Iowa - Majestic Theater Chicago, Wilson Avenue Theater
22 Indianapolis, Indiana - Lyric Opera –
December
6 Pittsburgh, Pennsylvania
20 Brooklyn, New York - Bushwick Theater
27 New York New York America

Original Creole Orchestra Itinerary – 1916; January–December
V= Variety F= Indianapolis Freeman, B= Billboard, D= Chicago Defender

January
3 ¼ Town Topics opens in Boston, Massachusetts
24 Town Topics New York, New York
31 Town Topics New York, New York
February

7 Town Topics New York, New York
14 Town Topics Detroit
21 Town Topics Cincinnati, Ohio [Sun opening 20-26]
28 Town Topics St, Louis [opens 27-4]
March
3 Town Topics Chicago, Illinois [sold out]
13 Town Topics, Chicago, Illinois
20 Town Topics, Chicago, Illinois
27 Town Topics, Chicago, Illinois
April
3 Town Topics, Chicago, Illinois
10 Town Topics Columbus, Ohio
24 Town Topics, Pittsburg, Pennsylvania
May
1 Town Topics, Cleveland, Ohio
8 Town Topics, Cleveland, Ohio
15 Town Topics, Buffalo, New York
22 Town Topics, Philadelphia, Pennsylvania
29 Town Topics, Philadelphia
July
3 [Chicago, Illinois in transit]
17 Winnipeg, Canada
24 Edmonton, Canada
31 Calgary, Canada
August Canadian Pacific Line South
7 Great Falls, Montana, Orpheum (2 Ngts.) Missoula, Montana (2shows Thur.) Anaconda,
Montana (2shows Fri), Margaret Meade Theater Til 16
21 Spokane Washington [sold out]
28 Seattle, Washington
September
4 Vancouver Canada
11 Victoria, Canada
18 Tacoma, Washington
25 Portland, Oregon
October
9 San Francisco California [sold out]

16 Oakland, California
23 Los Angeles, California
30 San Diego, California
November
6 Salt Lake City, Utah
13 Ogden , Utah [6-18]
20 Denver, Colorado
December
4 Kansas city, Missouri, Pantage Theater - Sioux City Orpheum
11 Omaha, Empress Theater

Original Creole Orchestra Itinerary - 1917; January–June
V= Variety F= Indianapolis Freeman, B= Billboard, D= Chicago
Defender

January
1 East St. Louis Missouri, - Erber's St. Louis Missouri, - Empress
Theater, St. Louis, Missouri, Grand Theater
8 Chicago, Illinois Lincoln Theater [1st half]
21 Decatur Illinois Empress Theater– (WVMA)
21 Springfield Illinois Majestic, Theater Chicago Illinois Wilson Avenue
Theater (WVMA
22 Indianapolis Indiana – Lyric Opera, Chicago Illinois Kedzie
Theater(WVMA Davenport, Columbia (South Carolina Area)

29 Chicago, Illinois Lincoln Theater, Chicago, Illinois, McVickers
Theater, Palace Theater
February
4 Waterloo, Majestic Theater – Dubuque, Majestic Theater
5 Fort Wayne, Indiana Palace
11 Lincoln Nebraska, Lyric Theater - Theater Sioux City, Iowa
12 Rockford , Illinois Palace
18 St .Paul Minneapolis Palace Theater (Probably a week)- Diluth,
Minneapolis New Grand Theater
25 Minneapolis New Palace Theater
26 (Probably a Week)
March

4 Madison, Wisconsin - Orpheum Theater
11 Rockford Illinois, New Palace theater. Kenosha Wisconsin, Virginian
12 Milwaukee, Wisconsin Palace theater
18 Between April1 and March 18 Band was to show in Terre Haute Ind or St Louis Grand Opera House (No evidence they showed)
26 New York, Winter Garden Theater
April
2 New York, Loew's Orpheum Theater
9 New York, American Roof
May
7 Philadelphia, Gibson's Standard Theater (CVBA) Colored Vaudevill Benevolent Society
14 Philadelphia, Gibson's Stan
June
July
2 - 31 Orchestra Doubled (Lawrence Duhe Band-Ensemble Band -) (5 Weeks)
August
6 - 30 Orchestra Doubled (Lawrence Duhe Band-Ensemble Band -) (4 Weeks)
September
3 - 24 Orchestra Doubled (Lawrence Duhe Band-Ensemble Band -) (4 weeks)
October
2-14 Orchestra Doubled (Lawrence Duhe Band-Ensemble Band -) (2 Weeks)
15 Moline ,Illlinois Palace Theater
22 Chicago [Logan Square ? -] Palace Theater , Fort Wayne, Ind]
29 Detroit Colonial Theater
November
5 Detroit Colonial Theater
12 Decatur Empress
19 Chicago American - Chicago, Lincoln
26 South Bend Indiana, Orpheum Theater- Indianapolis Lyric Opera House
December

3 Lafayette, Indiana Family
10 Muskegon Regent - Kalamazoo Majestic
17 Battle Creek Bijou - Jackson Orpheum
24 Lansing Bijou - Flint Palace
31 Saginaw

Original Creole Orchestra Itinerary - 1918; January–June
V= Variety F= Indianapolis Freeman, B= Billboard, D= Chicago
Defender

(The Palao family returned from New York to Los Angeles and relocated to Chicago 1918. Anita Palao his fourth daughter with Agatha was born in Chicago 1918.)

January (Palao family in Chicago Anita born in March 7, 1918)
14 Danville Illinois, Palace Theater - Springfield Illinois, Majestic Theater
21 Chicago Illinois, Wilson Avenue Theater
28 Davenport Columbia - Waterloo Majestic
February
4 Dubuque Majestic
11 Sioux City Orpheum - St Paul Palace
18 Duluth Grand
23 San Diego Jelly Roll played - Creole Band [Dead Man Blues
25 Minneapolis Grand - Madison Orpheum [Sold Out]
March - (March 16, 1918 Last engagement)
4 Milwaukee, Wisconsin - Palace Theater
18 Kenosha Wisconsin - Virginian Theater, Evansville, Illinois - Grand Theater
25 Terre Haute, Indiana Hippodrome Theater – Elgin, Illinois
April
15 Chicago, Illinois
May
13 Chicago, Illinois

Jimmy Palao Band Activity July1918- 1928

July

28 Chicago, Illinois riot Eddie Vincent took Jimmy Palao and his family to train station July 28th 1919 to Milwaukee, Wisconsin. They left Milwaukee, Wisconsin the end of August to return to Chicago in time for school to start August

August

8/1919 Lawrence Duhe [1918-1919]

October,

1919 Jimmy Palao rejoined Lawrence Duhe, Band and World Series Game Leader Mutt Carey leaves Joe Oliver takes over and renames band early 1920 ,..King Oliver Creole Band (Chicago)

May

1920 Goes to California

King Joe Oliver Band [1919-1921] Jimmy in early 1920. After dispute with Joe Oliver Jimmy left King Oliver band in California 1922. He returned to Chicago, Illinois

(Dreamland closed May 1921 reopened after Jackson lend money to reopen)

John Wickliffe's –Ginger Band [1922)

Syncopated Gingersnaps [1922]

Dave and Tessie Band [1922-1922

References/Notes

Abbreviations

TOBA: Tough in Black Artist
WRC: William Russell Collection
WVMA: Western Vaudeville Music Association

Chapter 1....New Orleans the Home of Jazz [11-21]

I fell in love with New Orleans... the sounds of music, the people and the welcoming, southern hospitality, the smells of flowers, food and the tropical breezes. I hope this chapter conveys the love I feel for New Orleans as I talk about the birthplace of Jazz. Only New Orleans had all the correct elements to produce the music called Jazz.

Chapter 2....Jimmie Palao's beginnings; Descent, Legacy and Culture 1879...[21-40]

1. [* New World Encyclopedia – Miscegenation] [1] Felix Palao listed as slave in records and older picture [rootsweb. ancestry.com/~ilissdsa /text_files/database_intro_files /071601NQ.htmand]birthmothers name Delarossa. Could be first or last name, or first and last name such as; Dela Rossa nationality African. This explains Felix being listed as

a slave. Miscegation theory 'one drop of blood' this practice ended in 1920

2. ["Creole" By Sybil Kein 2000, Louisiana State University Press., Baton Rouge 70803] This is perhaps the best description of the Creole culture ever written. It is confirmed by Armontine Palao There is a list several books on the Creole culture State they all seem to contain the same information

3. Name book on Mother Henrietta Delille

4. Hernsheim Factory Largest cigar factory in USA

5. Church records list marriage of Edouardo and Madeleine

6. Historical Tour house where Jimmy Palao was raised

7. The 1860 federal census [Reference:, The Encyclopedia of African-American Heritage, by Susan Altman Copyright 1997, Facts on File, Inc. New York , ISBN 0-8160-3289-0] [3] Palao loved and cared for his son Jimmy Palao. He maintained a loving relationship with his granddaughters until his death in 1937. Natalie brooks his great granddaughter remembers when he would visit and she would sit on his lap and she said; she remembers he always smelled good. She never knew what kind of men's cologne he wore.

8. Armontine interview and Clotilde notes

9. After the Civil War, separate and unequal was the norm for New Orleans schools. In the 1878s -1910 funds from the estate of John McDonogh, a wealthy trader and slaveholder, began to be used to construct schools. For poor whites students and Black Americans students, In the same period, black students were routinely restricted to lower grades and had previously had no access to high school. Southern University first opened on March 7, 1881, in New Orleans, Louisiana, on Calliope Street. It remained there until 1883, offered academic studies beginning with the primary grades and extending through high school in 1912 moved to Baton Rouge in 1914 and offered study from sixth grade through two years of college. Until the 1920's St. Katharine Drexel

of Philadelphia and her Sisters of the Blessed Sacrament, a religious community dedicated to the education of African Americans and Native Americans, established Xavier as a high school in 1915. The four-year college program (BA) was added in 1924-1925 throughout the USA. McDonogh #35, the first black public high school in New Orleans, was opened in 1917 it remained the only black public high school until Booker T. Washington opened in 1942 [Gathered info - public domain]

10. 1900 Census Felix involved with Josephine sired two children Felicia 1892 and Norman 1897

11. Clotilde interview

12. Armontine interview
    Jimmy Palao leader of the Buddy Johnson Band is not to be confused with the Buddy Bolden Band. [William Russell collection Manuel Manetta, 3/21/1957.Reel IV of 6 - Digest-Retyped, Armontine interview

13. Charles love interview **(WRC)** WR Collection, Bacage Interview. Probably the Pacific Brass Band
    According to Charles Love it was during this time that Jimmy Palao learned to play the saxophone. WR Collection, Charles Love Interview Reel 1- summary-retyped, 1/16/1960 pg 2- 3 Armontine Interview

14. Cumulative readings on Henry Allen again in snippets

15. [Jazz New Orleans 1885-1963 An Index to the Negro Musicians of New Orleans] Edgar Palao played several clarinet

16. [Ray Lopez, interview, Hogan Jazz Archive, Tulane University, , Reel III (transcribed excerpt on Buddy Bolden by Ralph Adamo), June 17, 1898 - August 17, 1898, Company B, Station of Company at San Juan Hill,; Samuel B. Charters, Jazz New Orleans, 1885, New York, Oak Publications, , pp. 7 & 15; John McCusker, interview,) Little is said about this curious and yet significant chapter in the New Orleans Brass Bands history. These bands were

territorial and if a Band marched into another's district a contest ensued creating a spectacle that drew crowds of delighted spectators. The instruments were put down and fist and knife fights ensued. Many were hurt and a few were killed.

17. The community at large was becoming concerned about the violence in these marching bands. They were becoming a threat to society. Politicians were becoming alarmed. The United States sent recruiters out to enlist these band members in the Spanish War. If they had continued to compete in violence. They would have self destructed and the music known as Jazz perhaps wouldn't exist (They all played Ragtime by Rudi Blesh and Harriet Jarvis

18. Edgar made his first and perhaps only theatrical road tour in 1904. Opportunities to join the traveling Negro companies were easy for a talented musician. A number of the companies originated in New Orleans. There was for example Bush' Opera Company a variety show that toured the South under the management of the New Orleans musician, Joseph Palao. It was discovered that Edgar Joseph Palao often used only Joseph Palao.

19. Recruiting of Spanish War Ninth Immune

20. Armontine interview

21. Recruiting Spanish War memories

22. Interview Claude Wright Reel

23. [Jazz New Orleans 1885-1963 An Index to the Negro Musicians of New Orleans]23

24. Cumulative from [Jazz New Orleans 1885-1963 An Index to the Negro Musicians of New Orleans]and Claude Wright and Armontine

Illustrations
Picture taken in Louisiana, Grandson, James Palao 1967
Felix Palao (1920), Rebecca Palao (1882). Family Album

House Jimmy Palao raised in 900 Verret, Algiers, New Orleans, Louisiana
Felix Palao Kneeling Next To Tuba, cropped (1917) Family Album
Henry Allen Brass Band (1898)
Ninth Infantry Immune Regiment in New Orleans (Spanish War) marching to board ship to Cuba
Illustrations: Pg. 38 Jimmie Palao Picture Taken Around 1920

Chapter 3, First Steps of Path to Jazz Career 1897

1. Cumulative Armontine St Cyr Interview , Old Mint information

2. Cumulative Buddy Bolden Louisiana State University Press, Baton Rouge, Louisiana, 1978, 176 pp It was said that Jimmy Palo taught Buddy Bolden how to read music.

3. Armontine Interview, Buddy Bolden Book

4. Scientific Findings It was said you could hear Bolden playing his horn ten Miles away. Scientific research from the Waters of Louisiana revealed it was possible to hear across the waters, 15 or more miles away. In the early 1900's there were no tall buildings and or phone and electrical wires to interfere with the air currents across the waters. (In Search of Buddy Bolden: First Man of Jazz).

5. Buddy Bolden Book

6. Cumulative Lil Hardin, Armontine

7. Rose and Souchon 1967, 164

Illustrations:
1900 - Jimmie Palao Band

Chapter 4....Played Jazz with Top bands 1900... [49-76]

1. Peter Bocage confirms that Jimmy Palao was the leader of the Imperial Band. Also on cap in picture of Jimmy Palao

with uniforms Leader is written William Russell Collection Peter Bocage, Reel 1 only

2. Ray Lopez interview agreed Jimmy Palao and Bill Johnson had formed a strong partnership.

3. Cumulative [Armontine Interview] and [St Cyr Interview]
Johnny St Cyr Interview Imperial band

4. Cumulative 1910 Census and Family Bible Armontine Interview Marriage

5. Armontine recollections A romantic at heart George hooker Interview

6. Jonathan Finkleman discusses bucket of blood dives...

7. [Storyville by Lois Battle] There were countless descriptions of Jazzville the section on the swamp Al Rose calculated that

8. The story of Buddy Bolden never takes away from the fact that Buddy is recognized as the Father of Jazz. (William Russell Collection, Eddie Dawson Reel 3]

9. Nothing to confirm black faces images as being accurate descriptions of the band.The band never made up in blackface. Prince Morgan did a performance similar to Al Jolson's performance in blackface.... The second part of his script was in tuxedo and top hat and singing and dancing Leonard Scott.

10. [Hear Me Talking To Ya, Lil Hardin Armstrong]

11. [Don Heckman in The Oxford Companion to Jazz],

12. [Coming Through Slaughter by Michael Ondaatje, author of The English Patient]

13. Armontine Palao; Interview]

Illustrations:
1905 Jimmy Palao (Uniform) 1905 Imperial Orchestra
1905- Imperial Orchestra (Suits),
1905 Milneburg Picnic cropped from

1905 Milneburge Picnic
1908 Jimmy Palao on the Riverboat… On the mightyMississippi
1908
Jimmy Palao and Freddie Keppard

Chapter 5…First to Coin Term "Jaz" / The Original Creole Orchestra 1908

1. [Encyclopedia Britannica] Definition Jazz
2. Evidenced business cards
   The variations of New Orleans Jazz were tough to play. The tempos were difficult and there were lots of key changes, which made the music difficult for others to play; even those who could read music they still couldn't mimic this New Orleans Jazz style. This explains why the Jimmie Palao's business card states Creole. It was a selling point because Creole musician were in high demand in Los Angeles, Chicago, New York because of their reading skills and/or ability to play New Orleans Jazz… [Jimmie Palao, J. Singleton, Copyright 1976]

3. [(Armontine interview] Jimmy always called Music Jazz from the day she met him in 1905. Armontine said Jimmy taught Buddy Bolden how to read music.[Armontine interview]
4. Armontine and Clotilde interview]
5. Jean Christopher Averty's notes
6. Bill Johnson Interview
7. In 1908 James Palao and Bill Johnson formed a firm partnership. Bill Johnson and Jimmy Palao registered and founded the Original Creole Orchestra in June 1908. Baquet Interview Other sources
   (Picture from Defender 1911) This poster picture from Jazzmen confirms the picture existed in 1911. I have a date of 1909 as the original date of the picture. The tuxedo with white shirt and white and scoop vest was stylish between the years of 1890-1920

8. According to Robert Goffin in his book (LaNouvelle Capitale Du Jazz) Jimmy Palao sent telegrams to the men for them to join them in California

9. The unfortunate forms of racism caused this band not to continue travel across the Dixie Line. Little did they know the dangers they avoided because they later discovered that in some southern states there were Jim Crow laws to lynch and kill any one of mixed blood. (Jazz a History of Jazz)

10. Bill Johnson Interview Booking gigs and expertise Barbary coast

11. Chicago Defender[Picture from Defender 1911] [Jazzmen]

12. Cumulative Los Angeles and Creoles well educated

13. [Armontine Interview)separation

14. Manuel Manetta Interview Easter Massacre

15. [Armontine Interview) Palao Pleads to return home

16. Contradiction on lottery concerning Armontine

17. [Dink Johnson Reel III WRC]voodoo beliefs sometimes strange people or warnings appear Eddie Vincent on train

18. [Armontine Interview] Ed Dawson interview confirms Jimmy Palao as best violinist

19. Armontine Interview

20. Robert Goffin; Palao sent telegrams

21. Bill Johnson letter in regards to white skin tone

22. There was mention of cutting contest and supportive evidence found in [Cutting contest Wikipedia encyclopedia]

23. Cumulative list of books Pantage offer and fight Leach-Cross

24. Edgar Palao funeral

25. [Paul Howard Interview] how great they played.

26. Confirmed in Several books and writing the character of summarized after reading several books

27. Imagined Jimmy Palao's walk might be like the Denzel Washington walk or Billy Dee Williams strut

28. Palao Style

29. Porterfield Josh direct statement on rehearsals and directing of band

30. Techniques that they individually were credited for using.

31. Pantage tour

32. Exploring Early Jazz] [Such A Melodious Racket, The lost History of Jazz In Canada 1914-1949]

33. [French Book]

34. [WRC Collection]

35. [Pioneers of Jazz by Lawrence Gushee]

36. [Paul Howard Interview]

37. [Jimmy Palao, J Singleton1962]

38. [Jimmy Palao, J. Singleton, Copyright 1976/

Illustrations
Jimmie Palao and Dink Johnson
Picture of business card from family album sent to Clotilde from Al Rose. [Al Rose supplied a copy of 1908 business card to Clotilde Palao-Wilson]
Picture of business card Creole from family album (1910)
Poster Chicago Defender 1911, Original Creole Orchestra
Picture of business card from family album (1914)
Jimmie Palao Chicago Historical Society Saxophone and Banjo,

Chapter 6.... Gained National Prominence 1914 ... Broke barriers

1. Exploring Early Jazz] [Such A Melodious Racket, The lost History of Jazz In Canada 1914-1949]

2. Common Knowledge all book state this information [James Palao- J.Singleton1976}

3. Collective improvisation was nothing like heard before

4. It was Jimmy Palao along with other band members who first heard and accepted lil Hardin into the band. She was the first African American to enter the field of jazz and become a major figure and to retain that position throughout her career. the first woman to successfully enter the Jazz field

5. Chicago key Jazz spots

6. Union local 208

7. Band excited the crowds

8. Bill Johnson interview

9. Paul Howard interview

10. Town Topics tour shook the rafters

11. John Underwood interview

12. Review of 1914 muddled and confused

13. Review Henry Morgan Prince, performed Blackface makeup. They say he introduced new dances such as the ball in the Jack and Charleston.. There is a mention of Mable Elaine in Black face playing the Town Topics with her ragtime band. December 1916 let it be understood she never played with the Original Creole Orchestra. They were with Orpheum circuit in December 1916. They were perhaps a replacement after The Original Creole Orchestra left Town Topics. Its apparent they weren't successful they were never heard of again.

14. Baquet left The Original Creole Orchestra. I couldn't find a satisfactory explanation. Big eyed Delille took his place after being turned down before

15. Seattle News

16. Oregon Daily

17. San Francisco Examiner

18. Original Creole professionally trained

19. Keppard couldn't read but was a virtuoso. He had remarkable range the music he played 89 years ago sounded like modern Jazz today

20. Palao respected these Jazzmen's musical talent.

21. Lil Hardin Gave the best description of Keppard.

22. General and descriptive information on band member found in snippets from interviews and books. There was not enough information to give anyone any specific credit for.

23. Summarized information in several books on William Manuel Johnson

24. Armontine Clotilde interview on Jimmy Palao she states that as a Jazz musician, he was the only one of that era that encompassed traits to lead this band.

25. Lil Hardin speaks to hot violin playing

26. Anonymous interview and WRC collection

27. Charles love speaks highly Jimmy Talent

28. Eddie Vincent and St Cry speak of travels

29. Bill Johnson didn't book across the Dixie line only once in South Carolina…

30. Work was plentiful for the musicians

31. Bands and or band members played with other band to keep the cash flow going on off times or just to make more money

32. Palao took family responsibility serious

33. Pops Foster interview on good times together

34. Sofia Tucker always took an interest in new music from black songwriters.

35. Jazz broke racial barriers brought races of all classes and gender together. The racial mixing seen around America was remarkable

Illustrations:
Creole Orchesta 1909
Jimmy and Mable 1915

Chapter 7.The Ups and Downs and The Prolific Years of Jazz 1918…]

1. Storyville closed, Marcus Loew Contract

2. Keppard offered recording deal by Victor representative not too likely

3. 3. **[William Russell Collection interview with Bill Johnson Reel** #] I read the over reels from the William Russell Collection interview with Bill Johnson and found the following overlooked statement; "Bill Johnson had an interview with William Russell 12/19/1938 Bill Johnson mentions; that possibly another record offer was made to

him by Victor. He says it came through Bill Vodery. He was a leading Negro arranger in Chicago. In the interview he states that Bill Vodery could be found c/o Handy Music Company." This is the first reference I have found to a representative's name and to any contact being made with Bill Johnson... Bill Russell lived 100 years and their seems there were very few if any other interviews done with him. I and another scholar concluded that " Vodery might have learned of the opportunity for a Black touring orchestra to make a record for Victor, and passed on the opportunity to Johnson." perhaps that started the conversation between Keppard and all of the band members that states they were against recording. It makes better sense because Bill Johnson was the manager of the band and would have been the only one to handle all business matters transactions. Bill Vodery was a very important figure in the music world. He was an African-American composer, conductor, orchestrator, and arranger, and one of the few black Americans of his time to make a name for himself as a composer on Broadway, working largely for Florenz Ziegfeld.

4. Record recorded "Tack Em Down" not issued

5. Chicago Played jelly Roll martin Ist Time Playing with Jimmy Palao Original creole Orchestra (Dead Man Blues Jelly Roll Martin Way Out West) ("Hear Me Talking to Ya "by Nat Henoff)

6. Compositions by Jimmy Palao rare for this era

7. Keppard drinking got to train too late with tickets. The band missed gig in Boston

8. Death of Scott Joplin

9. Lawrence Duhe Original Creole set in and approved of Lil Hardin and accepted her into the Lawrence Duhe Band Played together five months

10. Returned to Original Creole band to complete engagements.

Letter from Original Creole band to editor of Chicago Defender This letter is a source of pride. It shows strength of character. and they certainly present a united front. They had to be strong and tough to have successfully remained in the entertainment business for these long number of years. Leonard Scott is listed as the bands comedian in letter dated March 6, 1918. However October 27, 1917 states Leonard Scott, formerly of the Dahomian Trio is now with the Creole Band, where he will introduce Charles Warfield's song "From Now On Let Me Miss You.(IF)"(Such A Melodious Racket, The lost History of Jazz In Canada 1914)

11. Cumulative accounts

12. Armontine recalls conversation to disband

13. Declared king of Kings of Jazz"

14. Palao in 3/5-1918 in Chicago when Original Creole Orchestra disbanded went to work with Lawrence Duhe Chicago riot Vincent took Jim and his family to train station July 28th 1919 to Milwaukee

15. They left Milwaukee end of August to return to Chicago in time for school to start

16. Jimmy Palao never lacked work

17. Lawrence Duhe 10/5/1919 World Series game Lawrence Duhe had the honor of leading the first Jazz Band to Play at a World Series game. It was the Cincinnati Red Sox versus the Chicago White Sox series of 1919. [Shining Trumpets by Rudi Blesh Louisiana Life Series: No 3 Second...1919]

18. Lawrence Duhe died Sugar Johnny died 1918 Mutt Carey replaced him 1919 Jimmy was asked to rejoin in August 1919 and Joe Oliver was in the band, (first time Joe and Jimmy worked together. Mutt Carey resigned Freddie left and warned Jimmy about Oliver took over and a few weeks later named band the King Oliver King Joe Creole band.

19. Jimmy goes to California with King Oliver Band 1921 with a six month contract June 21- December 21

20. Recalled by Floyd and Buster Wilson Assumed the master copies were melted during shipments across desert. King Oliver Band recorded under Sunshine Label in 1921

21. Oliver disposition, Oliver suffered Health and dental problems

22. Armontine disappointed with how they were dressed.

23. Armontine and Clotilde recalled Jimmy's argument with Oliver and how Oliver treated Jimmy. Many arguments ensued between Jimmy Palao and Joe Oliver. Their styles were different and Jimmy didn't like the way Joe Oliver always upstaged everyone They remained angry about Oliver letting their father go without notice Jimmy left King Oliver band in California 1922 He returned to Chicago

24. Afterward Armstrong joined band Bill had a booking for a show in Chicago

25. Lil Hardin and Louis Armstrong married Feb 23, 1924. Jimmy at wedding. Joe Oliver and Bill Johnson were not present.

26. Milwaukee Journal

27. Chicago Tribune

28. Facing the cold in Chicago

29. Jimmy Palao reinvents himself.

30. Pictures contributed by Modesta Palao

31. Johnny St Cyr remembers Palao sitting in for Piron and Piron walked away from the Olympia Band the incident remembered by St Cyr could have been that Keppard and Palao set in for a one night gig with orchestra in 1917. They were in between bookings at this time and both went on to The Lawrence Duhe band mid May 1917 until mid October 1917. Keppard and Palao returned to the Original Creole Orchestra to finish the bookings before disbanding the end of 1918.[St. Cyr Interview

32. Race Records

33. Jazz Cardinals names given Freddie Keppard-cornet, Eddie Vincent-trombone, Johnny Dobbs-clarinet, Arthur Campbell-piano, Jimmy Palao-violin, Jasper Taylor-wood blocks, Papa Charlie Jackson-Vocal Salty Dog.

34. The digitally re-engineered records allow us to hear how they sounded.

Illustrations

Jas Palao and daughter Agatha 1917
Lawrence Duhe August 1919 Cosmisky Park Creole Jazz band Jazz Band [
Dreamland Café, Lawrence Duhe Band 1919
King Oliver band Poster Black and White 1921
John Wickliffe Band
Jimmy Palao picture taken around 1920 [5-29]

Chapter 8.....The Last Days of Jimmie Palao 1928 [169-184]

1. Jimmy Palao hits the big

2. Variety Dave and Tressie [W.R. Collection; Charles Love]

3. On road with Dave and Tressie Bill notified Jimmy was sick.[W. R. Collection; Eddie Dawson] ,[Pops Foster;][3], Ed (Red) [WR Collection]

4. Armontine Interview [WR Collection]

5. Eddie Vincent accidental death

6. Meets daughter Modesta and grandchildren

7. We do hear the sounds of Jazz just as he wished,

8. Witness to Jazz Royalty

9. Lil Hardin gives good account of Jimmy and Montudi Character

Illustrations:
Syncopated Gingersnaps 1921

Syncopated Gingersnaps 1922
Jimmy Palao and Eddie "Montudi" Garland 1922
Postcard Dave and Tressie 1922
Two buddies Eddie Vincent and Jimmy Palao

Chapter 9....Sounds of Jazz in Memory [185-201]

All events and people are set in place for special souls to enter this world at a certain place and time. They follow a direct path and no matter what the circumstance they can't be stopped until their mission is complete. They go against all the odds. Everything is suddenly set in motion, the correct people and the right moment and with a driving force they have an lasting impact that will bring a change in the world. We have witnessed this phenomenon time after time.

Epilogue
Epilogues are like the roots of a tree that are always in bloom
This historical account is just the beginning of many truths to be unearthed.
Reference End notes
"It is in the quiet crucible of our personal private sufferings that our noblest dreams are born and Gods greatest gifts are given, in compensation for what we've been through." Wintley Phipps. God told him to share this with the world.

Index

Carey, Jack 16, 29
Carey, Mutt 29, 99, 162, 176
Celebrate over 100 years of Jazz! 132
Celestine, Papa 29
Chicago Conservator 76
Chicago Defender Newspaper 70
Chicago Historical Society 132
Chicago, Illinois xi, 28, 43, 46, 48, 51,
    52, 53, 54, 55, 57, 63, 65, 68, 69,
    70, 71, 72, 76, 78, 79, 82, 83, 87,
    89, 91, 92, 93, 95, 96, 97, 98, 99,
    100, 102, 103, 104, 105, 107, 109,
    112, 114, 116, 130, 132, 135, 136,
    138, 139, 140, 142, 143, 145, 146,
    149, 153, 154, 155, 156, 157, 158,
    159, 160, 161, 162, 169, 170, 171,
    172, 175, 176, 177
Chicago Tribune 104
Chicago Whip 76
City of Music 4
Claire, Frances 68
Clark, Walter xi
Club 101 Ranch 36, 55
Club Cadillac 55
Code Noir 2
Coleman, Claudia 68
Collins, Lee 122
Collins, Wallace 16, 29
Congo Square 2
Cookie. *See* Palao, Armontine
Cook's Dreamland Orchestra 109
Coycault, Ernest 47, 48, 137, 154
Creole community 3
Creole culture 4, 164
Creoles 3, 11, 49, 53, 122, 170
Creole tradition 14
Crescent City 3
Cutie Blues 121

D

Dave and Tessie Band 28, 162
Dawson, Ed 57, 131, 170
Dawson, Eddie 29
Deluxe Café 92, 98, 143

Depression 85
Dixie 18, 50, 137, 149, 154, 170, 174
Dobbs, John 100, 143
Dreamland Café 70, 99, 178
Duhe, Lawrence 28, 30, 83, 92, 98, 99,
    142, 143, 145, 148, 149, 160, 162,
    175, 176, 177, 178
Duson, Frankie 15
Dutrey, Honore 29, 98, 100, 101, 143
Dutrey, Sam 29

E

Early, Frank 55
Economy Hall 4, 106, 142
Eddie Dawson 144, 168, 178
Edmonton, Canada 67, 68, 155, 158
Elysian Fields 32
Excelsior Band 14, 79, 125

F

Family Bible 14, 35, 168
Ferrand, Madeline 14
Ferzand, Alphonse 48
Field, George 30, 98
Filhe, George 30, 31, 33
Foundation of the French Colony of
    Louisiana 53
Frank, Gilbert\"Babs\ 30
Frank, Robert 145
French Quarter 2, 6, 23, 49, 121
Friedlander, Lee 130
Friends of Hope Hall 4

G

Galloway, Charlie 30
Garden District 6
Garland, Ed \ 30, 111
Garpard, Vic 30
Geddes Hall 4
Glenny, Albert 30
Goffin, Robert Jazz scholar 59, 91, 92,
    131, 170
Good Intent Hall 4